LETTERS
FROM
THE PIT

Stories of a Physician's Odyssey in Emergency Medicine

DR. PATRICK J. CROCKER

Print ISBN: 978-1-54395-332-9

eBook ISBN: 978-1-54395-333-6

To my wife, Marcia, and my daughter, Alison.
Without their unfailing support my career
would not have been possible.

PRAISE FOR LETTERS FROM THE PIT

A raw, unflinching look at one of the most bizarre and stressful occupations a person could choose. Dr. Crocker takes us through his career in emergency medicine, serving up one fascinating case after another. He writes with the vulnerability of someone keenly aware that they don't get it right every single time. His honest, often humorous insight into medical education and practice is a refreshing departure from the norm.

Travis Pipkin, RN, MSN,
Emergency Nurse Practitioner

Dr. Crocker is one of the godfathers of emergency medicine in central Texas, and I was fortunate to learn from him as a very green new attending physician at Brackenridge and the Children's Hospital of Austin. "Brack" and "CHOA" have been replaced by Dell Seton Medical Center at the University of Texas and Dell Children's Medical Center, where Pat Crocker's legacy of excellence is alive and well in all of us who served under him in "the pit." He tells these stories so well the reader feels like he is looking over Pat's shoulder as he unveils the mysteries and oddities of the emergency department. His recollections stir the memories of any emergency physician, some great, some terrible, all impossible to forget.

Letters from the Pit made me feel like I was right back in the middle of the ER action again. It brings what happens behind the scenes in the ER into focus from a new perspective inside the mind of the physician. A very enjoyable read.

In a culture of comic book heroes, it's gratifying to be reminded that there are real heroes out there. Everyday the staff of Emergency Departments throughout the world are there saving lives 24/7/365. Pat Crocker provides us an intimate glimpse into the growing mind of an Emergency Physician, from residency through a fascinating 37 year career. The stories are poignant, instructive and hard to put down. A great read.

Letters From the Pit is a searing emotional account from the front lines of medicine. As Dr. Crocker relates his courageous stories, of the lives he saved or lost, we come away with a vivid portrait of an emergency physician, seeking to do the best for his patients, one shift at a time. I highly recommend this riveting story of loss and hope in the world of medicine.

Letters from the Pit is a wonderful example of elegant storytelling. Dr. Crocker explains through poignant prose the thoughts, emotions, and challenges of the emergency physician. Happy, sad, horrific and thought provoking moments from his career. Physicians are not often open about their failures along their path, but he shares it all. The book is an excellent selection for anyone interested in reading good stories, doctors, nurses, medical students and residents everywhere. A series of stories that is captivating and will keep you wanting more.

Don Connell, M.D., retired Emergency Physician

Letters from the Pit reveals a physician›s journey to find balance between help and harm, empathy and self preservation. The «in-the-moment» writing style provides insight into the emotions and thought processes that occur in the midst of life-changing moments for patients, families and care givers. These stories reveal the appeal, rewards and costs of Emergency Medicine. We see evolution and growth seep through as a physician, a human being, is changed one case at a time by life events, as all of us are.

Sharon Long, M.D., Emergency Physician

In a very real way, Dr. Patrick Crocker combines powerful stories of life and death situations in the ER with common sense reflections on the over-medication of America and what should be done about it. You will be right there with him as he practices his unfailing devotion to "first, do no harm" in the day-to-day drama that is the emergency room.

JoAnn S. Dawson, award-winning author of
the Lucky Stable Series and Bed, Breakfast and Beyond

Dr. Patrick Crocker uses his lifetime of stories from the most vulnerable place of all, the emergency department, and summarizes them in beautiful, chronological prose pulling the reader into this exciting world. Patrick lifts the curtain for the reader to see a different and unexpected side of life in the emergency department that portrays life-and-death medical situations with lyrical meditations on the world of medicine and the world at large. This little gem contains knowledge and lessons that can be applied not only in the medical field, but also in personal life. I found this book of personal vignettes to be a refreshing and exciting change in what I'm used to when reading medical emergency stories.

COL (ret) John McManus, M.D., SPEAKER,
American College of Emergency Physicians

I SINCERELY HOPE YOU ENJOY THIS BOOK. THE BOOK HAS BEEN INDEPENDENTLY PUBLISHED SO THERE ARE NO MAJOR PUBLISHERS INVOLVED, AND NO FORMAL PROMOTION OR MARKETING. I AM DEPENDING ON THOSE READERS WHO LIKE THE BOOK TO SEND A RECOMMENDATION TO FIVE OF THEIR FRIENDS. IT IS THROUGH YOUR CONNECTIONS ON SOCIAL MEDIA THAT YOU CAN HELP GET THESE STORIES TO INTERESTED READERS.

LET YOUR FRIENDS KNOW THE PREFERRED SELLER IS THE BOOKBABY ONLINE STORE [bookbaby.com]. IT IS ALSO AVAILABLE on 50 OTHER ONLINE STORES.

THANK YOU.

P.C.

TABLE OF CONTENTS

FOREWORD

All medicine began as emergency medicine for one had to survive the acute to consider the chronic, but the discipline only grew into a medical specialty 50 years ago. This is what makes Dr. Crocker's essays so engaging for emergency physicians. They are both deeply personal reflections of what it is like to be in "the pit," awash in blood, tragedy and dark comedy and also a chronicle of most of the lifespan of the specialty itself. Surely, they have broader interest to anyone seeking the catharsis of tragedy, of seeing it happen and feeling the rush of relief that it is not happening to you (though it might someday). Dr. Crocker tells these stories in simple and compelling prose accessible to a wide, non-medical audience, but, at its heart, it is an emergency physician's tale. It is about the saves you try to remember, the losses you try to forget and the toll it inevitably takes.

Primum non nocere is a noble aspiration at least as ancient as Hippocrates and a sign of wisdom in the practice of medicine. The human body is often quite adept at healing itself if we don't get in the way. Dr. Crocker illustrates how it can be a guiding principle, but sometimes you have to do something. In this, Semper Paratus or "be prepared" might be a better motto, one Crocker also uses in the bizarre and surprising confines of Austin's safety net hospital, Brackenridge.

When he arrived in the 1980s, he was one of few physicians board certified in the nascent specialty of emergency medicine. He set about making the changes that would help grow Brackenridge into a respected academic teaching center, Level 1 Trauma Center and eventually the primary teaching hospital for Dell Medical School at the University of Texas at Austin. To those of us emergency physicians who arrived over the following decades, he was the boss, granted, one in Birkenstocks (and cargo shorts when he wasn't on shift, scrubs when he was). He led from the front, an excellent clinician and role model.

Prior to medical school, I spent a decade covering tragedy for a metropolitan daily newspaper -- conflicts, hurricanes, homicides, tornados and plane crashes, but it was always an experience once removed. The emergency department was the shock of the thing itself. Learning to stay calm and think in that environment is the near impossible task emergency physicians and staff face everyday. But as Dr. Crocker's poignant stories illustrate, it can be done and done well. The art and science of medicine can be brought to bear in the chaos and frequently save someone's life.

The old Brackenridge stands empty now, condemned, soon be demolished to make way for a shiny new office tower. The new hospital was built just across 15th street on the University of Texas campus. And though many of the same docs still practice in the new ED, it's hard not to look at the old blue and white tower without a tinge of nostalgia. Austin's medical community began to flower there, much of it under Pat Crocker's watch. It is a special pleasure to relive some of those Brackenridge stories in this collection of essays guided by an Austin institution, Dr. Patrick J. Crocker.

Truman J. Milling Jr., M.D. – Austin, Texas, October 2018

PREFACE

I trace the genesis of this book to a long drive I made after earning a master's in Human Nutrition from Cal Berkeley to Des Moines, where I would enroll in medical school. I planned to write a series of letters to my great college friend, Jack, about my experiences. Jack and I met during undergraduate orientation at Berkeley and became fast friends, roomies and later, housemates during my two years of graduate school. Jack not only encouraged me in my studies, he was innately curious about medicine so I knew he would be interested my letters. Jack majored in biology, and became a highly regarded science teacher and cross country coach. I knew I could tell Jack anything. No judgment.

I imagined dutifully chronicling my passage through Des Moines University's College of Osteopathic Medicine, my subsequent residency, and eventual practice in emergency medicine. In my drive East from the California Bay Area on Interstate 80 some of the vast desolate areas of Nevada, Utah and Southern Wyoming seem to naturally produce a meditative state. I considered my future, the impact of leaving all of my family, friends and relatives, and what that meant on a personal level. I thought of Jack and knew that the close friendship I had hoped to sustain was unrealistic now given the geographic separation. I wondered what I could do to keep it alive.

I envisioned writing to Jack in a first-person, stream-of-consciousness narrative of my life as a doctor. What I saw and what I was thinking in real time as I treated patients. No self-censoring. Perhaps one day, the letters could be bound into a book for family and friends. They would understand some of the challenges I encountered and why I found emergency medicine endlessly fascinating.

As it turned out, I did write some letters, though not nearly as many as I thought I would. None was sent. Life, the rigor of training and practice, all got in the way.

Over the years, I had transitioned through a parade of computers and various iterations of word processors. Most of my letters to Jack were lost in an unrecoverable format. Just why I didn't save paper copies is beyond me. I'm happy to say that our friendship has endured.

As I approached the end of my career in emergency medicine in 2017, I rekindled my interest in assembling the letters into book form. Jack and my family might get them after all. Perhaps a broader readership would have an interest in my stories, the ones I could never forget. Emergency medicine, after all, has been a common theme of TV shows as it so often skirts the thin line between life and death, miracles and tragedies.

And so, after I retired, I began to reconstruct some of the notable cases of my career. These were the cases that shaped me and sometimes haunted me. All are actual events during my career. They are presented in approximate chronological order and roughly span the period from 1979, my senior year in med school when students do hands-on patient care, to 2017. The letters, I hope, will bring the reader into the world I inhabited for nearly four decades, all in Texas, at Darnall Army Medical Center at Fort Hood; Brackenridge Hospital and Dell Children's Medical Center, both in Austin; and Peterson Regional Medical Center in Kerrville. I spent the vast majority of my career as medical director of the emergency departments at Brackenridge and Dell Children's. Those hospitals are the highest-level trauma centers in the Austin region, and many of my most memorable experiences took place alongside a gurney in a trauma room. I recreated most of the text from my memories so quotes may not be exact. Identifying details of patients have been changed or omitted, and a few minor details have been changed to further protect patient confidentiality. Any resemblance to persons living or dead resulting from these changes is purely coincidental. The names of those providing the medical care have also been omitted.

A recurring theme in these stories is the concept of "primum non nocere," Latin for "first, do no harm." It is the ethical principle on how physicians are to treat their patients. This phrase, while elegant in its simplicity, is incredibly complex and sets up one of the basic tensions in medicine. We are trained to save lives and tend to look on patient deaths as some sort of defeat. Nowhere is that truer than in the emergency room where seconds count, fast decisions get made, and patients often live or die because of what we do — or perhaps, fail to do. Sometimes, saving a life means violating the principle of doing no harm. Finding the perfect balance becomes an almost-daily struggle. It was for me. I took the words, primum non nocere, to heart, although I would not grasp the full meaning of this seemingly straightforward statement until later. Now, after thirty-seven years of practice, I can say that while I tried hard to keep that promise to my patients, I did not always live up to it.

Before we descend into "the pit," a few words about the book's title. "The pit" is the nickname residents gave to the emergency room. Many of us felt like our ER shifts were spent in a pit below the Black Hole of Calcutta, an eighteenth-century dungeon that was especially deadly to its occupants. And, for certain, there were shifts that felt like that.

I have read a number of books by other ER physicians and trauma surgeons detailing their experiences. Some said they came to feel their souls were stained, as the stress of practicing emergency medicine bled into their personal lives. Searches for solace that sometimes ended in drug or alcohol abuse. These accounts sadden me. My experience, on the whole, was profoundly different.

I recall the deep satisfaction that came from being trusted by so many thousands of patients. Helping people in their time of need. Solving medical mysteries with only tiny nuggets of information. Stretching my skills to save lives. Those days were, quite simply, a joy. Of course, there were bad days. Days when help was elusive, when patients died, despite our best efforts. Days when I did not fulfill the great promise I held dear.

But even on my worst days, I would never trade my career. Not for anything. For me, practicing emergency medicine was living my dream. And I got to live it with the finest group of emergency physicians and nurses I can imagine. My entire staff, from doctors to clerks, always strived to deliver the best care at the highest professional level found anywhere in Texas. We formed a tight-knit group, standing by 24/7/365 and had each other's backs. Always, we put our patients first.

And I got to do it all in the most comfortable attire: scrubs and sandals. What could have been better?

PC

MY FIRST DELIVERY

Dear Jack,

"I don't know nothin' 'bout birthin' babies." No quote could be more apt. I just finished my Obstetrics and Gynecology (Ob/Gyn) rotation. First month on the wards and I am delivering babies. What a neat experience. Actually, it can get pretty messy. I never will consider giving up my amateur credentials in gynecology, but delivering babies is something else. Nice, young patients for the most part, healthy babies delivered to smiling parents. Lots of happy endings. It is almost enough to make one consider doing it for a living. But as I said, I will keep my amateur credentials.

Picture this. It's seven in the morning and my first day on the Labor and Delivery floor (known in the hospital as L&D). I'm standing around waiting for the resident who's training me to show up and orient me to the service. As a senior medical school student, you don't dare start anything on a new service without an orientation and your resident's express permission. That would be stepping on the resident's turf. In addition, you know absolutely nothing about practical medical care. Your resident will tell you what to do and what not to do. That should keep you out of trouble most of the time. He or she will almost be as good at this as some of the older, experienced nurses by their second year.

You always meet with the nurses after orienting. That is, if you are smart. There is no scheduled meet and greet. It's not required, but it's essential for those with enough common sense to know you will need their help and wise counsel. Just admit you're clueless; they know it already. They can tell by looking at you. They know you're as fresh out of the box as your clean, white shoes. Valedictorian or class dummy, you don't yet have a clue about real-life medicine, and the nurses can smell it. A few well-spent minutes with them, a cup of coffee or two, and you can become golden. They will keep you out of trouble. Many of the residents never learn this little courtesy and they will constantly be watching their behinds as they recover from screw up after screw up -- all of it preventable. A good nurse can be your best friend, or your worst enemy. The sooner you understand that they are the other half of the care team and that you can't do your job without them, the better off everybody will be.

At any rate, I hadn't had the chance to seek out any of the nurses yet. Nor was that in the cards today. Within a few minutes of my arrival in L&D, I heard a loud cry for help from down the hall.

"Help, we need a doctor in seven!" someone shouts. My immediate response, of course, is to run to the phone and call one. A doctor, that is. I am serious here. I don't know anything practical about birthing babies. I did see a video about a year ago, but I've never witnessed a birth in person. Just like reading about sex as a Boy Scout in a tree house. It isn't much like the real thing, and neither is a video for delivering babies. Again, a piercing call from that relatively young voice for help.

I'm not a doctor yet, OK? A doctor is someone who knows the answers, can help no matter what, a wellspring of self-confidence and knowledge. I am still just me. I feel no different than the day I graduated from high school. Oh sure, I've learned quite a bit about Ob/Gyn pathology, physiology of reproduction, embryology, etc., but nothing of any practical value for this situation. I may as well be a plumber. I'd probably still be warm and cozy in bed if I were because plumbers don't work on weekends, and this is Saturday. I really want to run the other way, but you know me. I can't. So, I run down the hall to find a young nurse and a frantic patient in one of the labor rooms.

These are small rooms with regular beds where women suffer the first part of labor. Then when it is time to deliver, they are moved to the delivery room. Deliveries are supposed to happen in delivery rooms, not labor rooms. I guess nobody explained it to this patient because there she was, splay-legged on the bed with something bulging from her vagina. It kind of looked like a pale, yellow balloon about four inches across. I've never seen anything quite like this. I'm wondering silently if her guts are coming out. The nurse, not knowing whom she is dealing with, looks up expectantly and says, "Doctor, she is about to give birth." Well I'd pretty much figured that part out all by myself. I still want to call a doctor and stand in the background and watch one or two of these before I actually do one. At any rate, I am *it* this morning, and all I can do is try and deal with the situation until an RD arrives. RD stands for real doctor. In the firmest most authoritative voice I can muster (though probably not very reassuring), I say, "I'll need the precip tray." This is a tray all set up with what you need to do an emergency, or precipitous, delivery. I'd learned that much from the video, and in times of need, my memory usually doesn't fail me. Of course, the nurse is one step ahead of me. She points out that the stainless-steel tray now positioned at my patient's left leg was indeed the precip tray. So much for bluffing.

By now, the nurse has figured out I am just a new intern or maybe even a student who's making this up as I go along. Nevertheless, in front of the patient, I am the doctor, and she is the nurse, and there is no question about our role-playing. I should have thanked her later for that little bit of courtesy because, without it, the charade would have certainly crumbled right there. The resident is still MIA, and my heart is beating so fast I wonder if it's going to hop out of my chest. But I have no luxury of time, so I pull on gloves and a mask. No time for a gown. That mysterious bulge is growing with each contraction like some obscene balloon.

I get down close trying to figure out what to do next when, whoosh! Slimy water gushes onto my face. A bucketful. No joke. I am disoriented and surprised, and as nearsighted as I am, it takes a second to register that her bag of waters has ruptured, douching me in the face and covering my glasses. I can barely see through this coating of amniotic fluid. I am clearly in deep shit. Where in the hell is the frigging resident?

Somehow, I can still remember a few simple steps from the video and successfully guide the baby's head outward. Fortunately, the baby is in the common LOA, or left occiput anterior, position. Textbook. But now I am panicked. The baby looks like a monster. Or maybe a gremlin-like mobster wearing a nylon stocking mask. The mouth, eyes, and nose are visible, but a thick membrane covers the entire head and face. What am I to do? I can't suction the baby's mouth because there is no hole to get to it. I don't even know if I should let this baby survive, it is so deformed. What will I tell the mother, or for that matter, the dean of the medical school? "I'm sorry, sir, my first baby was deformed, and I didn't know what to do, so I let it die!" I figure my career in medicine is over. I suppose if your first patient dies, surely, you fail on the spot. After some humiliating medical grand rounds where some gray-bearded expert lecturing in an auditorium explains your incompetent buffoonery to your colleagues, you probably get shipped back to where you came from. Maybe I can learn a trade; I've always kind of liked the idea of carpentry. I already imagine telling my parents and wife that, starting next week, I will be framing condos in Orlando. But thank goodness for Mother Nature.

She has saved me and every other physician from making many a blunder. Another contraction comes, and if by magic, I have the shoulders out now and, lo and behold, the awful membrane peels away from the baby's face, and it looks normal! My God, thank you. I will be a doctor yet. All the fuss was over the amniotic sac that, once in a great while, will cover a newborn's face. Turns out this unusual event has a name, a witch's veil. This wasn't covered in the video. I give a slight tug, and out slides the baby. Slippery, but just fine. Someone hands me a cord clamp. Snip, a normal-looking baby. Yahoo!

I'm a doctor with a patient and my first baby. I am ecstatic. The newborn's loud wailing is sweet to my ears. The mother is happy, the baby is fine, and the nurse has quit screaming for a resident. Another contraction, and there is the placenta. Just like the video. And I order ten milligrams of Pitocin to control bleeding after childbirth. Just like the video.

I must have looked a little better than I felt because smiling in the doorway is an older nurse who looks like she was around for Hippocrates's delivery. She simply says, "Good job." She has been there the entire time, watching me, protecting her patient, the baby, and protecting me. She won't let a dangerous error occur. She doesn't intervene as she sees things are going well. She understands that I need to learn to crawl before I can walk, walk before I run. She knows I will stumble along the way but the best way for me to learn is by doing just what I am doing. Hands-on care. Fall. Get up. Learn. Try again. She has been involved with probably thousands of trainees during her career. Nurses like her are priceless.

Baby, mother, and young nurse go off to the nursery. The older nurse and I take a few minutes to reflect on the scene. I am still wiping amniotic fluid off my face. It is on the floor, the wall, and I am soaked. What a picture. Suddenly the tension is gone and behind closed doors the two of us laugh until we cry. I've found an ally, and the truth cannot be hidden. The real pecking order has been established. She watched out for me for the rest of the rotation and made sure everybody knew what a good job I had done with my first delivery. She saw to it that I got first dibs on any delivery I wanted. You see, Jack, if you can swallow your pride and accept help, which you do need, and understand medical care is a team sport, a good nurse can be your best friend.

On the final morning of the rotation I hunt up my new nurse-friend to thank her and say goodbye. I find her at the nurse's desk. I tell her that I'm grateful and that I start my pulmonology rotation after lunch. She says, "Oh, you will do fine, young man." I turn to leave and hadn't taken five steps when

I hear her say, "I mean, you will do fine, Dr. Crocker". I turn back for a last smile and go on my way. She knows I am not a doctor yet, and so do I. Soon, though. I won't forget this little compliment, this courtesy, ever.

I decide there is no need to walk to my new rotation. I will simply float.

PC

A DAILY DOSE
OF EXHAUSTION

Dear Jack,

How goes it, my friend? I'd like to say not much is new here because I could use a little routine in my life. But a residency does not permit a routine. After two years of being up all night every third night and eighty- to ninety-hour workweeks, you don't know how good working nine to five sounds. This total lack of disregard for the body's normal biorhythms is exacting a toll.

The first day in the rotation is not too bad. You wake up refreshed and feeling pretty good. Morning ER rounds are over by 7:30 a.m. You know what you face, though. You won't be headed home again until tomorrow at 5 p.m. That is roughly a thirty-four-hour shift. If I get an hour of sleep during the shift, I will be lucky. I thought the usual workweek was supposed to be forty hours. You learn to conserve your energy.

After ER rounds in which you check on patients throughout the department, morning work rounds are next. This is the time you go through the wards checking on all of your patients. See how they are doing, order new labs or treatments, whatever they need. You have to listen to their lungs. You see, if you don't listen to their lungs, they don't think you're truly taking care of them. Doesn't matter what is wrong. Could be a leg infection. But they all want to know, how do my heart and lungs sound, doc? Frankly, I don't care. I listen, though, and nod. "Sounds great today," I say. It's the same in the ER. You learn that moms and dads believe a good, thorough doctor must look in your ears, check your throat, and feel the glands in your neck. Again, it doesn't really matter what their chief complaint is. You do these things for the patient and family. After all, that is what we are all about. Many of my friends have yet to figure this out. I hear them defending themselves to the chief resident. "I don't know what they're upset about. The baby had an ear infection. What good would feeling their neck glands do?" They just don't get it. Save a life rarely, cure occasionally, but comfort always.

As part of the ward rounds, you review each patient's chart, the vital signs, and the nursing notes. Then, you go see the patient. You make decisions about their care plan for the day, or even possible discharge. About 10 a.m., your boss, the attending physician, comes in, and you do the rounds again. This is what you see on TV. That cluster of doctors in white coats going from bed to bed and receiving the wisdom of the attending. You present each patient and their problem in a capsulized version, summarizing their life and current problems into a few sentences. It is superficial, but if it's not done in a caring fashion, it comes off as crude to your patient.

You don't want that. This is your patient. You may have spent an hour or two the afternoon before taking the person's admitting history and physical. You try to develop rapport. You care about them. They are your responsibility now. But your attending doesn't care about that. He or she wants it brief, to the point, and if possible, looking to link prior lifestyle indiscretions to the patient's current problem. They made themselves sick, right? Not really, but if we attempt to take ownership of their problems as unavoidable, we realize we may, and in fact will, suffer a similar fate one day. We try and forget that we are vulnerable to the same afflictions as our patients. Otherwise, it's too stressful to worry daily about your liver, your kidneys, your heart. Every resident or student imagines they have at least one fatal disease during their training. But acting impersonal seems to be the key to being viewed as a knowledgeable young resident.

During rounds with the attending, I introduce him to a forty-five-year-old man who presented with chest pain yesterday. His EKG was normal, but his pain was characteristic of heart disease. He has smoked heavily for years and rarely exercises. His labs are OK today, and we will put him on a treadmill tomorrow. My patient's past indiscretions have caught up with him. For the patient, it must seem like a trial: Guilty as charged. You are hereby sentenced to heart disease because you were a bad boy the last twenty-five years. You're getting what's coming to you. We'll do our best to help, but don't forget you did this to yourself. An added bonus for all of us: This won't happen to us because we don't smoke. The attending is pleased. Next patient. One of our older residents, a smoker, visibly pales. He realizes his future link with this patient, this disease.

By the time we finish rounds, the ER is starting to call. We've got new patients. The call for an ER consult always seems like a bother when you are on the wards. You have work to do, a schedule to stick to. How dare they interrupt you. They have no schedule, of course. No one controls the flow of patient arrivals. If you're sick or even think you are, you come. But the interruption during ward rounds somehow makes it OK to be rude to your buddy in the pit. Can't he mind the store while I'm busy? Inexplicably, the resident you were working side by side with last month in the ER, the same one who helped you decide what a seemingly mysterious rash was (poison oak), is now a dummy. A buffoon. Unable to make the slightest decision without an internal medicine consult.

And the consult is the grandest farce of all. Because in most every teaching hospital the first consultants are trainees too. Your internal medicine consultant that day may be the family practice intern rotating in with no experience beyond their basic training. Bizarre. For patients sick enough to be in the hospital, this is what they get. The intern. It ought to be the attending. I've always been a believer in giving it your best shot the first time around. But this is not how medical education works. The attending will see the patient tomorrow. In the meantime, we depend upon nature, good luck, and our own limited experience to see the patient through till morning attending rounds the next day.

At 5 p.m., you're done on the wards. Time for a quick bite to eat, and then an all-nighter shift in the ER. Then, you do ER rounds at 7 a.m. the next morning and head back to the wards. The ride home won't start until 4:30 p.m. I will be exhausted. A quick dinner with my wife, a little TV or Atari, and then I will collapse into bed.

And so it goes. One full day bleeding into another.

PC

THE PECKING ORDER

Dear Jack,

I'm finally getting my feet on the ground, learning the skills I will need to survive in this place. It seems like forever since we first talked about going to medical school, and now I'm finally in the hospital learning how to practice medicine. I found the first thing I had to master had nothing to do with medical care. It was the pecking order. Never step out of your place in the hierarchy or you could be pecked to death.

The Medical Student - A hospital's pecking order is very stratified and highly developed. Medical students are, of course, at the absolute bottom. They are considered the lowest of life forms by everybody except the occasional bored little old ladies who are unwittingly grateful to see a "doctor." After a few weeks of life at the bottom you feel about as welcome as a street alcoholic in the ER at 3 a.m., moaning about a stomachache.

Medical students spend their days moving from one unpleasant task to the next. The resident's term for this is "scut" work. Scut work comes in two forms - that which is highly unpleasant, such as unnecessary rectal exams on routine admissions, or some other highly boring activity of no clear value to anyone, such as the detailed admitting physical on a healthy twenty-five-year-old who has nothing wrong except a hernia. One of the staff doctors refers to us as "scuts" because all we can do is scut work. Another calls us "wedges" after the simplest tool known to man. If the more senior residents can think of some new scut for you to do, believe me, they will. Being a senior resident means never doing scut yourself or saying you're sorry for making someone else do it.

At the beginning of each month, the rotations change and you are assigned to a new senior. You can save yourself a lot of scut by impressing the resident as to how much you know. This is however a dangerous endeavor. If you are wrong, the scut work doubles. If you are smart, you read every night about the kinds of cases you saw that day in the hospital. And unless you are CERTAIN of an answer to a pimp question or are directly asked, KEEP YOUR MOUTH SHUT. Realize that you know next to nothing. You learn to listen intensely.

"Pimping" describes the "quizmanship" used to fine-tune the medical staff hierarchy. Think of it as an inquisition possibly followed by a public flogging. It basically consists of asking the next lowest man on the totem to recall the most arcane medical fact you can recall yourself. Although frequently humiliating, it dangles the chance to leapfrog up the totem pole. If you can answer the question that the intern has missed AND can quote some reference article, it is a home run in the game of pimpmanship. Frequently, a whole month's grade may be scored by one successful response while the attending is present. Some pimpmanship is meant to be an attempt to aggressively demote you down the totem pole. You have to be careful.

I think you'll appreciate some excerpts from my favorite humor piece about resident life. It's comes from **How to Swim with Sharks: A Primer** by Richard Johns and is a magnificent description of my life now.

Swimming with sharks IS the reality of medical practice in a teaching hospital. Mastering this skill will be of importance.

FOREWORD (From How to Swim with Sharks, a dinner talk given by Richard Johns, circa 1974. It appeared in Transactions of the Association of American Physicians 1975;88:44–54. Excerpts are reprinted here with permission of the American Association of Physicians.)

Actually, nobody wants to swim with sharks. It is not an acknowledged sport and it is neither enjoyable nor exhilarating. These instructions are written primarily for the benefit of those, who, by virtue of their occupation, find they must swim and find that the water is infested with sharks.

It is of obvious importance to learn that the waters are shark infested before commencing to swim. It is safe to say that this initial determination has already been made. If the waters were infested, the naive swimmer is by now probably beyond help; at the very least, he has doubtless lost any interest in learning how to swim with sharks.

Finally, swimming with sharks is like any other skill: It cannot be learned from books alone; the novice must practice in order to develop the skill. The following rules simply set forth the fundamental principles which, if followed will make it possible to survive while becoming expert through practice.

I'm going to interrupt here to give you a little more explanation regarding the hospital totem pole and how it relates to the rules of swimming with sharks.

The Intern - a first-year medical school graduate. Barely higher up the chain than the students, with just enough perceived status to dump on them. Remember this law of physics: Shit ALWAYS runs downhill in hospitals. Never mind that some fourth-year students have a more sophisticated book knowledge of medicine than the interns. This can create havoc on the rotation. If you are stupid enough to correct the intern in front of others, you can consider this an automatic increase in your assignment of scut. If you know the answer when the intern is being "pimped," KEEP YOUR MOUTH SHUT!

The intern who utters the phrase, "In my experience..." is an absolute fool and destined to swim with the bottom feeders. The statement will earn a stare of absolute disdain from those above you. He has no experience, and thus, the statement is ridiculous.

OK, on to more shark-swimming advice from Richard Jones.

RULES

1. **Assume all unidentified fish are sharks. Not all sharks look like sharks, and some fish that are not sharks sometimes act like sharks. Unless you have witnessed docile behavior in the presence of shed blood on more than one occasion, it is best to assume an unknown species is a shark.**

2. **Do not bleed. It is a cardinal principle that if you are injured, either by accident or by intent, you must not bleed. Experience shows that bleeding prompts an even more aggressive attack and will often provoke the participation of sharks that are uninvolved or, as noted above, are usually docile.**

3. **Admittedly, it is difficult not to bleed when injured. Indeed, at first this may seem impossible. Diligent practice, however, will permit the experienced swimmer to sustain a serious laceration without bleeding and without even exhibiting any loss of composure. The control of bleeding has a positive protective element for the swimmer. The shark will be confused as to whether or not his attack has injured you and confusion is to the swimmer's advantage. They begin to question their own potency or, alternatively, believe the swimmer to have supernatural powers.**

4. **Counter any aggression promptly. Sharks rarely attack a swimmer without warning. Usually there is some tentative, exploratory aggressive action. It is important that the**

swimmer recognize that this behavior is a prelude to an attack and takes prompt and vigorous remedial action.

5. Some swimmers mistakenly believe that an ingratiating attitude will dispel an attack under these circumstances. This is not correct; such a response provokes a shark attack. Those who hold this erroneous view can usually be identified by their missing limb.

The Resident – this is two or more years after medical school. Suddenly, you have arrived when you become a resident. You are now looked up to by the nursing staff and have at least two levels below you to do your scut. Even if you were a lousy intern, and there are plenty of these, the nursing staff suddenly sees you as valuable. I don't know why. Upper-level residents who are exceptionally knowledgeable can frequently become as highly regarded as a first year fellow; the next rung up the totem. Residents have real experience and understand how to guard their posterior flank when the sharks are feeding, as the next rule indicates:

6. Get out of the water if someone is bleeding. If a swimmer (or shark) has been injured and is bleeding, get out of the water promptly. The presence of blood and the thrashing of water will elicit aggressive behavior even in the most docile of sharks. This latter group, poorly skilled in attacking, often behaves irrationally and may attack uninvolved swimmers and sharks.

7. No useful purpose is served in attempting to rescue the injured swimmer. He either will or will not survive the attack, and your intervention cannot protect him once blood has been shed.

The Surgery Resident - this is a unique subset of residents that for some reason consider themselves superior to the medical residents. Nobody knows why this is. They are frequently unable to answer even the simplest medical pimp questions. I guess their saving grace is they are so macho. I mean, they actually cut people open! (I however have always considered medicine residents superior, though, as they work their magic without cutting people open. That's a seemingly higher service to the patient, if you ask me.) Nevertheless, the long-standing position held by the surgery residents is "a chance to cut is a chance to cure." They're never in doubt but frequently wrong. And the surgical resident is often the master of anticipatory retaliation.

8. Use anticipatory retaliation. A constant danger to the skilled swimmer is that the shark will forget that he is skilled and may attack in error. Some sharks have notoriously poor memories in this regard. This memory loss can be prevented by a program of anticipatory retaliation. The skilled swimmer should engage in these activities periodically and the periods should be less than the memory span of the shark.

9. The procedure is essentially a sharp blow to the nose. Here, however, the blow is unexpected and serves to remind the shark that you are both alert and unafraid. Swimmers should care not to injure the shark and draw blood during this exercise for two reasons: First, sharks often bleed profusely, and this leads to the chaotic situation. Second, if swimmers act in this fashion, it may not be possible to distinguish swimmers from sharks.

The Fellow - This is a doctor who has finished his residency and is now specializing in some specific field of medicine. The fellow is highly regarded by all involved with medical care and is always trying what was described in the latest journal. They generally are too busy to get involved in pimpmanship. For the critically ill patients, a fellow is often their savior. A good one can simultaneously teach you, save patients from your misadventures, and buy you lunch at the end of the rotation! A good fellow is a master of hospital rounding strategy and often only speaks when it is time to expose the stupidity of those below him on the totem pole. The fellow fully understands swimming with sharks and the value of diversion. The good fellow will divert medical conversations that stray from his or her area of expertise.

The proper strategy is diversion. Sharks can be diverted from their organized attack in one of two ways. First, sharks as a group, are prone to internal dissension. An experienced swimmer can divert an organized attack by introducing something, often minor or trivial, which sets the sharks to fighting among themselves. Usually by the time the internal conflict is settled the sharks cannot even recall what they were setting about to do, much less get organized to do it.

It is scarcely necessary to state that it is unethical for a swimmer under attack by a group of sharks to counter the attack by diverting them to another swimmer.

The Attending - Considered minor deities by all trainees and most of the nurses. They steadfastly believe just one "real" doctor is now on the scene. Experience is worth a lot in medicine, so some of the adulation is warranted. I would usually choose a gray beard over a fellow, though. Even though they are usually less well-read than a good senior resident or fellow, their experience is often worth gold. The nurse will just do whatever they want. But don't ask them any pimp questions. They might not know the answer, and they really don't give a damn. And of course you will suffer. Remember the hospital rule of gravity.

OK, so now you know how the staff stacks up. As a lowly resident, I will have to watch where I dip my toes.

PC

FIGHT AND FLIGHT

Dear Jack,

ER patients come in two flavors, obviously sick and not so sick. It never ceases to amaze me the things that people will come to the ER with, feeling perfectly entitled to be there. I would estimate that a third of these people simply don't belong here and merely tie up people and resources, making it more difficult for my crew and me to take care of the really sick ones.

These not-so-sick patients often come with a unique perspective. Like the woman who had a rash for TWO YEARS and finally walks into the ER at 3 a.m. on a Saturday. This makes no sense, right? When I asked what brought her in at this particular time she said, "Well, I've had it for two years, don't you think it's about time something should be done about it?" You might think, as did I, "Hey, why not wait just one more day and see your own doctor?" But common sense is in short supply in the ER. Reminds me of that famous quote from **Mark Twain**: "I've found common sense ain't so common."

Today, though, I have no doubt about my patient. This little girl is sick. Even my relatively novice resident's eye can tell that. Two-year-old girls simply do not come in this shade of gray. By now, I've had my feet wet and know what we must do: We must resuscitate her. She's semi-conscious, confused, and struggling against us. This is not uncommon. It seems that the sickest patients are the most confused and combative. It is almost as if nature is saying, "This one is too sick to save. Back off," and then does everything possible to make our job more difficult. The patients yank out their IV's, can't hold still for X-rays, and fight our every touch. It takes four people just to hold down this little girl! Her temperature is 105. I do a quick lumbar puncture, and I am shocked by what I see. Normally, spinal fluid is crystal clear, like fresh spring water. This time, I literally get pus from her spinal canal. I've never seen anything like it. Of course, I haven't seen much yet, but something tells me it will be a long time before I ever see spinal fluid this strange again. As it turns out, this toddler had been intermittently seizing at home for the past twelve hours. I mean, talk about a parent with a high threshold to call a doctor. One patient waits on a rash for two years before seeing a doctor, and another has a family that keeps a baby home during twelve hours of losing consciousness, shaking, and jerking from seizures. There is no sense to this.

We control her seizures with a combination of phenobarbital and phenytoin and take her up to the pediatric floor. But she is too ill to stay in my hospital. We will have to move her from Fort Hood to San Antonio, where the medical center has a pediatric intensive care unit. This will require a helicopter flight late in the afternoon, with no chance of getting back before 9 p.m. Being the low man on the pediatric totem pole, I am elected to accompany her.

Oh, no problem, I am assured by my boss, the attending physician. Her seizures are controlled, and we have started antibiotics, he tells me. Besides, "Don't be stupid," he barks. "This little girl is going to die no matter what we do." I know in my heart that this is true, but I just can't approach children that way. No matter what. If you're eighty and have terminal cancer, I get that. But if you're a happy two-year-old playing in the yard one day and the next day you're comatose with a spinal column filled with pus, that's another horror show entirely. I can't accept this little girl's fate without putting up a fight.

I argue with my attending about putting her on a ventilator for the flight. He says no. I say yes. I've got a million reasons. She may seize again on the helicopter. That would be difficult to control on the helicopter. Having an airway will be one less thing for me to worry about. But, of course, the attending, who will be staying behind and probably watching the evening news while I do my futile best to help save this baby, wins. No intubation. No ventilator. "Just take the resuscitation bag in case you need it," he says. "But you won't." I manage to coax from him a quick review of appropriate drugs for seizures, cardiac arrest, and shock. And then, it's time to go.

Down on the pad, the chopper waits. I never flew in a plane until I interviewed for medical school, and I'm not too wild about the idea of riding in a helicopter. To make matters worse, my chief of service (residency director) is waiting to send me off with confidence on my first Medevac. He tells me not to worry, this is what I was born to do, take care of the sickest people. And oh, by the way, don't worry about the fuel fire on the helicopter. It was put out rapidly and did not damage the craft's ability to fly. What? A fire! On my helicopter? He sees I'm shaken and takes delight. He says, look, it will be OK. Just make sure they show you how to put on the parachute before they take off. Oh, and don't let them pull that old "new guy" trick on you. Everybody gets a parachute.

By now I've figured out there was no fire. Just his way of having a little fun at my expense. And even though this is a twenty-year-old Vietnam-era Huey that looks like it's going to crash doesn't mean it will. This is not the first time I find myself wondering: Am I in the right business? I mean, here I am with a critically ill toddler, flying off on an ancient green helicopter AND I have to worry about a parachute! I could be at home sipping an iced tea after a day of teaching high school. Oh, well. Off I go.

I notice to my relief that everybody on board seems competent and knows what every switch and light means. The whole damn helicopter is nothing inside but some canvas seats, with walls and a ceiling covered with instruments and gauges. We are just flying to San Antonio, a fifty-minute flight, but it looks like we could easily be going to the moon. I am impressed. These guys must have trained for fifteen years to fly this. Commercial airline pilots always seem to be about fifty, the picture of self-confidence and wisdom. Well, my pilot turns around to welcome me and I think he can't be much older than fifteen. This guy is probably still a Boy Scout. I'm not sure he even shaves yet. In fact, after a moment's reflection, I am sure that he has never shaved. This must be a joke. In a voice I'm sure cracked with fear I ask him if he is the pilot. Well, sure, he says. "I've been flying these things for six months now." Great. Fucking great. I want to ask how many of those months were without training wheels, but this is Fort Hood's Army hospital, so, I restrain myself.

For now, I will stick to the business at hand. I ask about the only thing on my mind right now, and that is, "Where is my parachute?" I also don't want to die without at least a fighting chance. If the helicopter is going down, I figure my chances with a parachute are at least better than nothing. All you do is just pull the cord and hope for a soft landing. Maybe a broken ankle or something because I have no training, but I'm game. I can do this. All I want is a chance to survive this doomed flight. My kingdom for a parachute. Well, the crew just collapses in laughter. I turn crimson and realize I've been had again. There are no parachutes on helicopters. We either land safely or we don't. It's just how helicopter flying works.

I have greater worries about my patient. We're about forty miles out, somewhere over Central Texas when my worst fears come to pass. The baby starts seizing again. I use the carefully rehearsed doses of Valium, and the seizure stops. She is hooked up to an EKG so I can monitor her heart, but the vibration is terrible on a helicopter. The readout looks erratic. And her pulse? I can't even feel my own pulse let alone hers. Predictably, things get worse. Valium and phenobarbital in combination will depress breathing, a key reason I wanted a tube and ventilator BEFORE we left. Now all I have is this low-tech resuscitation bag. I place the device's plastic cover over the baby's nose and mouth and press the bag with my hand to pump air into her lungs.

Suddenly, her heart rate drops. I realize I will have to intubate my patient in flight. I've never done this before. Not in flight. Not on a baby.

Actually, not anywhere on anyone. Why is this happening? Normally, passengers don't talk to the pilot, but the crew can tell I'm shaken. I scream to the pilot that we have to land right now or the baby will die. Maybe he thought I said that I want us all to die because the steady comforting whump, whump, whump of the helicopter blades simply stops. Now, only an occasional soft whump sounds as we fall from the sky at a very rapid rate.

My stomach is not just in my throat, but everything in the helicopter floats for a few seconds. Shit. I was sure my pilot had forgotten some arcane fact of flying like "Leave the engine on at all times" because we are hurtling toward the earth like a boulder from a cliff. Later, I am told we came down 2,000 feet in just over one minute. This, my friend, is fast. I suppose a little adrenalin is good for the system in an emergency. I think my adrenal glands have emptied out. I surprise myself and intubate the baby without difficulty somewhere in a cow pasture about twenty miles outside of Austin. The baby's heart rate comes up. She is stabilizing. I'm kind of proud of myself. Maybe I am in the right profession. At least I know I'm trainable.

But my victory is short-lived. Within a few minutes of lifting off, the baby's heart rate again slows, the term for which is bradycardic. I give atropine and epinephrine, but we lose her pulse. The corpsman and I perform CPR. Once again, a little victory. Spontaneous pulses returns. I ask for an abort to San Antonio so we head to the nearest hospital, which is Brackenridge, in Austin.

We soon land in a parking lot, and an ambulance takes us across the street to the hospital. This big-city trauma center is intimidating. The baby is whisked into a resuscitation room. I am not included. Within ten minutes, her situation worsens. Nothing more can be done. I can't believe the tragedy that has befallen this baby, my patient.

I call my attending to let him know that we lost her, and he is sympathetic. He simply says to come on back, leave the body there. I want to talk with the baby's parents, but they are somewhere unreachable traveling by car to Brooke Army Hospital in San Antonio. They still think we might save their little girl.

This is a new low for me. My first Medevac mission and all I have to show for it is a dead patient. I wonder for the second time in two hours if I will be able to do this for a living.

The flight back is sullen. I wonder if the crew knows how green I am, but they don't show it if they do. They simply say, "Thanks, doc," and leave me at the hospital helipad with a pile of equipment. I head home.

The next day, I seek consoling from my colleagues, but they don't really seem to understand the personal loss I feel. They say you did all you could, right? I say yes. No mistakes, right? I say no. You knew the baby was going to die anyway, right? Again, I say yes. But none of it matters. This little girl was my patient, and now she is dead. The death of a patient that you have empathized with fully is horrible. You have the illusion that somehow, it's your fault. You were in control and your patient died because you did a bad job. It is simply a feeling that cannot be shared.

I have nightmares for weeks afterward. I dream the baby has a twin on board who also is my patient. But in the dream, this baby also dies because I forget it is also under my care. I'm horrified. Now, I'm responsible for two babies' deaths.

I come to my first realization that a career in the ER is not survivable without distancing yourself from your patients. If you feel too much empathy, you also will become a casualty. I don't know how I feel about setting myself apart from my patients. I want to care for people, that's why I chose medicine. Now I've learned that I can't care about them too much. It's such a painful incongruity. How do you care for those you can't truly care about? Will I be able to walk this tightrope without faltering? I honestly don't know.

PC

A POWERFUL LESSON

Dear Jack,

    Sorry it has been a while, my friend. Two straight months in the intensive care and cardiac care units (ICU and CCU) has been all-consuming. I have learned so much, though. It is the perfect place and time to put all the medical science I've struggled to learn and the practice of real medicine together. Physiology and biochemistry simply fit into understanding what is really going on with these patients. Disease can and does result in some complex metabolic abnormalities, and it is fascinating to see them resolve with your therapy. At the same time, you learn a lot about people. And yourself.

    My first day on the ICU service, I am assigned a seventy-year-old man with a litany of problems that have rendered him quite fragile. The attending and senior resident assure me they will be at my side to guide me along. The patient will be my responsibility. Mine alone. I will see him two or more times daily, doing the necessary assessments. I will decide how to adjust his care and will be responsible for any next steps or procedures. At 10 a.m. each day, I will meet with them to review the case. With feedback from the attending and the senior resident, I will carry out the strategy I devise, with their blessing. And, yes, I'm on my own, but under their watchful eyes.

    For the remainder of the day, I will usually have one or two other fairly routine ICU admissions to cover. These patients may deteriorate but usually just need ICU care for twenty-four to thirty-six hours. I come to think of them as "the minor league patients." Their care is straightforward, and it gets simpler by the day. Diabetic ketoacidosis is now one of my favorite diagnoses for a relatively easy ICU patient. At 4:30 p.m., I will check out with the oncoming night team and review what I want done and the possible unanticipated problems they may encounter. From day one, my attending never interrupted or countermanded a thing. He sits quietly, listening and watching the senior residents react to my plans. This has been a confidence-building experience and continues into the final day of the rotation.

My patient is a mess. His whole problem started with a GI bleed. If that were his only active problem, he'd still likely be a minor league patient. In his case, things went from bad to worse. He bled enough that he had a heart attack. A week later, he had a severe embolic stroke, renal failure, and respiratory failure. Now, my patient is dependent on a ventilator. His metabolic problems are another long list. They include malnutrition after two-plus weeks of no food but trying to sustain a body churning out enough work for a daily marathon. A body trying to heal itself. All of this happened before I was assigned to care for him. And to amp up the pressure I'm feeling, he is a retired physician. Past chief of service at a major medical center. On the ventilator, he is uncommunicative, but his wife says to pull out all of the stops. He must be saved. I promise her I will do just that.

I spend the morning reviewing everything and trying to understand what I need to do to get him out of this downward spiral. After examining him, I think a big part of his lung problem is actually caused by his heart. He had a massive anterior heart attack, the worst kind, and it has left his heart so weakened that he is now in heart failure. He is holding fluid in his lungs that is preventing them for absorbing oxygen, and I think a special catheter that gets threaded through his heart and into a blood vessel in his lungs is his best option. I wonder, though, if all of his edema is from low blood protein or a weakened heart.

I go through all of this with the attending and chief resident. I cover all of the evidence from labs and other studies along with my exam findings.

The attending and chief look at each other for a moment. And then nod to each other. They agree with the plan. I'm asked if I have ever put in a Swan-Ganz catheter. No, I answer. I tell them I have done central lines before and have read how to thread this special catheter. I even helped with one Swan last month. My attending says, "Well, what are you waiting for? Get to work." Off I go. My chief resident will be sitting nearby charting and watching. He says, "If you have a problem, I am right here." This is the "see one, do one, teach one" philosophy at work. It's what teaching hospitals are all about.

It is hard to explain the combination of excitement, fear, and concern that sweeps over me. This is it. This is big-time. Once previously mysterious ICU medicine, and now I am doing it. Primum non nocere. First, do no harm. I am going to bring this patient out of the mess he is in. I'm going to do everything I possibly can for him.

He is awake but so weak he can hardly move. One side of his body is completely paralyzed from the stroke, but his intellect seems intact. I explain the plan to him, his wife, and the nurse. I believe he nods consent. Still intubated on a ventilator, he can't speak. He is too weak to write. His wife signs the procedural consent again asking that everything be done for him. After gloves, gowns, mask, hat, draping, and sterilizing skin are done, the procedure comes off without a hitch. I was able to establish central access with the first needle stick. Guide the wire in. Place the dilator over the wire. Take the dilator out and thread the catheter in over the wire. Take out the wire. The patient's blood carries the catheter through the right side of his heart and into his lung vessels. All the time, I am watching the pressure readouts confirming just where the tip of the catheter is. Balloon up and no pressure change. Advance a bit more. Take a pressure from the tip of the catheter. Holy crap, it floated right into what's called the perfect wedge position. I apply the dressings, remove the drapes, and cast off the garb I donned for the procedure. I've done it. Weha!

Every doctor has these moments of success and pride. Even joy. You have studied and worked so hard to get here, and now you have finally put your hands to work. And you find that you can do it. It's amazing. Not an ego trip but the culmination of so much preparation. The feeling is almost overwhelming. Every doctor will have these moments. This one's mine though. All mine.

I measure his cardiac output by flushing ice-cold saline in one port and measuring the temperature at the tip of the catheter. Combined with other measurements, I can estimate his cardiac output and learn just how well his heart is working. I do this every day. And always the arterial blood gas. Getting this blood sample can be difficult and more painful than a regular blood draw. They hurt. But I learn so much about his physiology. I am going to make him well, after all. It just has to be done. Some days, he cries. This is hard to see. After a few days, I place an arterial line so we can draw these samples painlessly. Maybe I should have done this the first day, I think.

I propose the new plan of care. We will use more diuretics to remove all of the excess fluid. We will continuously drip dobutamine I.V. to stimulate his heart muscles. Also nitrates to reduce the work on the heart. We will start a feeding tube and get his body making some protein again. The plan sounds good and satisfies me.

Every day, the same measurements and routines continue. I have removed about twenty-five pounds of fluid from him. His cardiac output has improved and his lungs have cleared. He has developed some decubitus ulcers, the technical name for bedsores that we are aggressively managing to keep from expanding or developing an infection. His lung X-ray nearly normalizes. We give him some progesterone that will help improve his respiratory muscles. Late in the afternoon, I get some respiratory parameters. These are measurements to see if he is really ready to breathe again on his own. They are satisfactory.

And, finally, after a month of work, it is time to remove the breathing tube. We call this extubation. You simply deflate the small balloon at the end of the tube and then gently slide it out. He is ready to breathe on his own and talk to us. I'll wait till tomorrow morning because sometimes we are wrong.

He could fail the trial and need to be urgently re-intubated. I don't want this happening in the middle of the night. Plus, a morning extubation will allow me to personally stand by all day. That's the plan.

Morning comes, and we've got a crowd. Two respiratory techs are in my patient's room with humidified oxygen and equipment for an emergency re-intubation. Two ICU nurses are here. My ICU attending is on hand. The patient's wife is here, too. I am thinking it will be a grand, happy moment after a month of countless hours trying to keep him alive. Maybe he will even finally be ready to move to the ward where he will be more comfortable. I explain to him what we will do. It is simple. I will deflate the balloon on the endotracheal tube and simply pull it out. He will cough a bit. Then, we will supply humidified oxygen for comfort.

That's exactly what happens. And it's done. The entire team is all smiles. I am still by his head reassuring him. And he tries to talk. A weak, hoarse voice, barely audible but not understandable. I expect a thank you. I crave that thank you. Nobody can hear what he has mumbled. I am right next to his head but need to get closer, my ear near his mouth. I ask him to repeat what he said. And with his hoarse whisper only into my ear I hear, "Fuck you." I must have paled, I was so shaken. The nurses ask what he said and I lie, "I couldn't hear him." The mask with oxygen goes back on, covering his face. I walk to the corner of the ICU and pretend to chart.

I am crushed. I don't understand. He wanted to live, didn't he? He couldn't communicate with us but his wife said, "Do everything, doctor." And, so, I did. And then it hits me. It feels like ice water has filled my veins. I am suddenly shaky. Primum non nocere has been my guide, but what have I done? Have I harmed my patient?

It dawns on me that he was ready to die all along. He never wanted to live after the crippling heart attack. He was ready then. And then the disabling stroke. Too weak to move. Bedsores. Kidney dialysis. Feeding tubes. So many needle sticks and procedures, all of which he hated. Even changing his dressings daily caused him pain. He has lain in bed all of this time, through everything, ready to die. He cried. Our only answers to him were more procedures. More pain. Oh my God, I think, what have I done? First do no harm, my ass. I have hurt this great man believing it was what he wanted. Listening to his wife, unquestioningly. And I only delivered pain. I feel shame. Very real shame.

At the end of the day, I say goodbye to everyone. I will be in the CCU next door for a month. Around noon the next day, one of the ICU nurses I had spent a lot of time working with on my patient comes over. She tells me our patient died quietly this morning. No re-intubation or resuscitation attempts. He has finally found his release.

I will never forget this case. Sometimes people are ready to die. It is just their time. They know it, and we must respect it. It is the cycle of our lives. From that day forward, I vowed I would always have the "How much do you want done?" conversation with my patients and their families. Do you want CPR? A ventilator? Do you really want everything done?

Most importantly, I remind myself, there is a time for everything, including a time to die. It's a valuable, but incredibly painful, lesson.

PC

To every thing there is a season, and a time to every purpose under the heaven:

A time to be born, and a time to die; a time to plant, and a time to pluck up that which is planted;

A time to kill, and a time to heal; a time to break down, and a time to build up;

A time to weep, and a time to laugh; a time to mourn, and a time to dance;

A time to cast away stones, and a time to gather stones together; a time to embrace, and a time to refrain from embracing;

A time to get, and a time to lose; a time to keep, and a time to cast away;

A time to rend, and a time to sew; a time to keep silence, and a time to speak;

A time to love, and a time to hate; a time of war, and a time of peace.

Ecclesiastes 3:1-8 King James Version

WHO SENT THIS PATIENT HOME?

Dear Jack,

I was working in the ER when the ambulance doors burst open, and EMS came in with a patient in severe respiratory distress. We had no advance warning as our encoder is up at the front desk, not back in the care area, and nobody gave us a heads up. I like to make sure the room is prepared and everything ready before such a patient arrives. Assemble the team in advance. Assign roles and some "must do" actions for each member. I believe it actually saves lives. But we have no such luxury today.

My new patient is flat on his back. He is breathing like a fish out of water, gasping for breath. Terminal respirations, I think. This is a unique breathing pattern. The patient is using his neck muscles to try to inhale air. It's largely ineffective in moving much air into the lungs. He clearly needs to be on a ventilator immediately if we are to save his life. But before we can even get him into our crash room he makes one last gasp and goes motionless. He has just had a cardiac arrest. Damn. Ten minutes ago, maybe I could have saved him. Now the picture is getting much darker.

Staff members are quickly filling the room, as happens with a critical patient. Suddenly, it seems like chaos. But it's organized chaos; everyone is doing something necessary. We get him on the bed and start CPR. I immediately start moving to get a breathing tube down his trachea so I can get him on the ventilator. His blood oxygen is certainly too low to try resuscitation without addressing this problem first. Laryngoscope in one hand and suction in the other, I am looking down his throat and am horrified. Not only is there a large pool of vomit there, partially blocking his airway and trickling down into his lungs, but when I slide the tube through his vocal cords and down his trachea yellow-green pus wells up into the tube. OMG, this is horrible and I know right away this is not likely to end well. I wonder when he was last awake and alert. Just how long did it take to deteriorate to this condition before he or his wife finally called for help?

We try the advanced cardiac life support protocols for about fifteen minutes, and I am getting nowhere. I need to go out for a few minutes and talk with his wife. Let her know we are still working, what we have done, that we are doing everything we can, but that things aren't looking good. I just can't break the news that he is dead without first giving her some warning. Give her at least a few minutes to adjust to the even more unwelcome news that is coming soon.

I also ask about events leading up to this. How was his health? How long has he been sick? To my shock, she says he was seen in the ER here just a couple of days ago. I am immediately silently furious. As the chief resident and more or less in charge of managing the other residents, I am wondering which of my residents saw this patient. Who came to the obviously erroneous conclusion to send this patient home? What an idiot! I try not to be openly critical, but she appears to detect from the look on my face that I believe something went wrong with the first visit. She tells me he was diagnosed with pneumonia, given a couple of prescriptions, and sent home. Goddammit. Could we have saved this man if he had had proper care the first time and been admitted? Why was he sent home? Who screwed this up?

Few things irritate me as much as mismanaged patients. Why didn't the physician fully think things through before sending this very sick man home? I am betting he didn't get proper instructions, either, on reasons to return to the ER. The chart will probably have only a few scrawled notes on it. One of my buddies or an attending in a hurry to catch up with an onslaught of patients has shortchanged this one, and now he is as good as dead. Goddamnit! Someone is going to get an ass chewing, and I'll be the one doing it.

I do not say anything aloud about this to his wife, of course. But I've already decided someone is guilty and I am going to find out who. Have a look at the chart and prepare to point out all of the mistakes this resident has made. Getting a chart from medical records takes at least thirty minutes so I ask the wife if she remembers the doctor's name. Maybe I can call the person down right now and let them declare this poor guy dead. That will teach 'em and maybe change such sloppy behavior.

She doesn't remember the name but says, "I have the medicines in my purse." Great. I suspect I've got the culprit and ask to see the meds. As she fishes around through her gigantic handbag, I am already planning just how this counseling session will be handled.

She hands me the medicines and I can't believe what I see clearly typed on the bottles. I probably turned visibly pale, as I'm aghast. I can't believe this particular doctor would make such a mistake. Send this man home. Give bad instructions. Because it isn't a friend's or an attending's name I see, it is MY name!

I am crushed. Thoroughly crushed. I didn't recognize him in his current condition, even though I saw him just four days ago. Yes, he had pneumonia. Two lobes of one lung involved, which raises the mortality risk much higher. I have been trained to admit such patients. The whole visit with him comes flooding back into my memory. I did tell him he needed to be admitted for care, but he refused. Said he would rather die at home than be in the hospital. I did tell him to return immediately if anything worsened, that even though we disagreed today about his going home he was welcome to come back and be admitted. None of these recollections help, though. He is dead, and I touched him last. I will be the one facing my director receiving the ass-chewing I was planning for someone else.

I am hoping I wrote all of this down on the chart. That the chart clearly records what happened that day. That I did everything I could for him without violating primum non nocere. I recall the admonishment during training that "if it isn't written down, it didn't happen." Going back and adding to the record at this point would be a horrible idea. Altering a medical record after the fact is not possible. Almost an admission of guilt, akin to forging a legal document. Did I fail this patient, I ask myself? Is he really dead at my hands?

I go back to the code still in progress and am absolutely morose. The STAT chest X-ray I ordered is hanging on the box now, and both of his lungs are completely whited out. This indicates every area of both lungs have become infected. The oral medicine I prescribed just did not work. I declare him dead. He has been flatlining almost since his arrival. We have nothing left to offer. Pupils are fixed and dilated. There is no hope after twenty-five minutes of CPR. I tell his wife a few minutes later and then complete the paperwork and death certificate. I feel sick to my stomach. And then the medical record from the prior visit finally arrives.

I take it back to my office to sit alone for a bit. Gather my thoughts and compose myself. I will still have to finish my shift no matter how lousy I feel. I still want to review the entire record and prepare my defense. As I look over the chart, I remember more details. I knew the patient needed admission and told him so. I recorded it all on the chart, thankfully. I even had him sign a special form entitled, "Leaving Against Medical Advice." And there it is, attached to the chart. I am a bit relieved to see all of this, but my mood remains dark. My chart is good, but my patient is dead. How did I fail him? Why couldn't I convince him to stay? What could I have done better? I am sure something could have been done, but I can't think of what it would be.

As I get up to walk back to the ER, I am reminded of something one of the ER docs said to me during my senior year of medical school. I was on my ER rotation. He said that here, you will have patients die at your hands. Are you ready for that? Can you really work in an ER knowing that will happen? You will fall, patients will die, and the question is, can you get back up? Do you really want to be an ER doc?

Today, I learned a powerful lesson. Never again will I be too critical of another physician's prior care without knowing all of the facts. Never will I make judgmental comments or expressions about another physician in front of a patient or the patient's family. I realize that although such behavior is pretty common among physicians, it is oh so very wrong. That second doctor who is being critical wasn't there the first time. Presentations change and things look different at a second visit. Time has passed, after all. Such comments hurt the patient's family, too. They don't need to feel worse than they already do. It is not fair commentary for anyone to make.

I decide I never want to be in this position again. Ever. And I am glad to have learned this lesson. And, yes, I feel like I have fallen, but I know what I must do next. I will get back up.

PC

WHAT THE HELL HAPPENED?

Dear Jack,

I never expected that my listening skills would play such a vital role in patient care. I suppose I was always too busy trying to master other areas of practice than to focus attention on honing this skill. At this point, though, it has become obvious how important it is to listen to the patient.

I have seen so many diagnostic errors made by physicians who failed to hear what their patients were telling them. I wonder why there is not a single course or even a lecture on listening and patient communication in medical school or residency. We are simply expected to develop this crucial tool on our own. This seems like a terrible omission from our formal training. Poor listening can and does lead to patient deaths, avoidable patient deaths.

Becoming a good listener is a more difficult skill than you might think. As is often the case, physicians themselves are the first barriers. We are trained to recognize that certain groupings of symptoms are characteristic of certain diseases. So, we strive to quickly collect symptoms and then plop them into a model of common diseases. We settle on the most likely disease that fits the patient's presentation and decide this is it. Eureka, I've got the all-important diagnosis. The patient becomes an 'x' on a form, neatly placed in their box, and we have already stopped listening.

Unfortunately, not every patient's complaints fit neatly into any box, no matter how hard we might try and force it. And this approach can simply lead to the wrong diagnosis, the wrong treatment, and the wrong outcome. There is even a name for this error: premature diagnostic closure. Once a conclusion is reached, it takes unusual discipline for physicians to recognize their error and acknowledge that they must start the process all over again to get it right. The error of refusing to budge from a false conclusion also has a name. It's called diagnostic momentum. Just when you really need to think the most, you get super-busy, and it seems everything is working against you, including the patients, who often communicate poorly. What I mean is most patients simply do not communicate very precisely. They are not purposely trying to be vague, misleading, or imprecise. They are simply trying to first tell you what they want you to know, what they think is important. And physicians prefer to do the opposite, i.e., extract the information they want to hear so they can push your symptoms into a little box. This situation sets up a built-in clash.

Some patients act like they don't want to answer your questions and will pull you down any number of rabbit holes. "What time did this symptom start?" I might ask. The answer might be, "Well, it was right after I got back from Wal-Mart." You then try another tack. "What time of day was that?" And they'll say, "Oh, that was right after Uncle John called." More knuckle-headed answers ensue before you finally extract a simple answer: 11:15 this morning. In the same vein, an essential question like, "Does this feel like your earlier heart attack?" will be met with: "I don't know, you tell me. You're the doctor."

Communication is often more difficult with older patients, the ones who are far more likely to have an important disease than a millennial or Gen Xer. They're usually not very ill at all. With them you can simply say, "What time did your mobile device say it was when your symptoms started?" They will consult Facebook, see what time they told their friends symptoms started, and answer "11:15."

Of course, the vital patient interview and listening is impossible with a two- or three-year-old child, and you must work through the parent's perceptions and concerns. It's the parental version of premature diagnostic closure. Almost every mom is confident she knows exactly what is wrong and will do her best to work you into a diagnosis that includes a prescription for an unnecessary antibiotic. Moms who have read too much on the Internet about the association of fever with the dreaded diagnosis of pediatric meningitis are not ready to accept that a thousand and one other things also cause fever. You must approach such a mom with caution if you are to care for her child properly. Sometimes, despite all odds and a ridiculous series of logical missteps, you discover, Whoa, Mom is right. So, you really have to listen and rigorously reconsider your own thinking or you'll risk violating primum non nocere. First, do no harm.

This particular morning would seriously test my listening skills. Like most shifts, we have too many patients and too little time to talk. On top of it, the phone's ringing constantly, and all of the calls seem to be for me. Lab, X-ray, consultants, and referring physicians are all calling today. One call is from the ER triage nurse, which is also not unusual if he or she is concerned about a new patient or simply wants to vent about a patient who should be turned away and directed to a clinic tomorrow with a minor problem. This time the call was about the latter. "Some mom is here saying her doctor sent them over because they think this three-year-old has meningitis. The kid looks happy to me. What do you want to do?" The nurse suggests just sending them back to the doctor's office. But when another physician has directed them to the ER, I am more cautious and ask the nurse to find a room for the pair. I will come and have a look for myself. There just is no other safe way to approach this scenario even with a happy looking kid. I'm feeling somewhat forced to interrupt what I am already doing so I can walk over to the frantic mom and her happy toddler.

Indeed, the child is playing with a toy and looks just fine, though he does have a low-grade fever. And Mom is in a tizzy. Obviously, something about the story doesn't fit so I call their doctor who tells me that their office is really full, and this mother was yelling about meningitis. They simply told her to go to the ER rather than take the time to deal with it themselves. This is called a "dump," and the ER doc is the unhappy recipient all too often. We have to suck it up and do what their doctor was unwilling to do. I bite my tongue attempting to conceal my growing anger with the referring physician. "Sure, I'll take care of them," I say. "Thank you." What I really want to do is deliver a terse lecture on medical responsibility and call them out as a lazy asshole. I go back to the patient room to an angry mom waiting in the doorway tapping her foot. Great. Just what I need today, an angry, panicky mom.

Mom has, of course, consulted Dr. Google and is now well informed that meningitis comes with a fever. Her child has a fever, and, therefore, he has meningitis. I can tell this one is going to take some time. When faced with this situation, I always force myself to remember I am a parent, too, and she is simply frightened and concerned about her child. It is all too easy to get sucked into their anger and frustration. A wise old doc once told me, "When the patient is loaded for bear, unload your own gun first." So, I carefully unload mine, taking care not to shoot myself in the foot.

I get a lengthy history and do a painstaking examination of this happy, healthy-looking child with a fever, largely to gain some credibility with this total stranger. I then move to talking about her son's care plan. She's having none of it. She simply will not accept the fact that a fever of 101.2 with a happy child is not a cause for alarm and likely is the result of a simple virus. She demands the all-important "blood count," which, she has also read, would be abnormal with meningitis. It's pointless to have a lengthy discussion about this test in this situation being totally unnecessary, so I relent and order the blood count. If nothing else, it will help Mom come to a little more ease over the situation. Plus, it's virtually harmless to obtain. And I order a urine test as well. As we part ways, I have gained credibility with her as a physician and am her new hero.

The blood count returns in about thirty minutes. It's normal, and I go back to deliver my reassurances that her son likely has a virus. Mom is now calmly watching a TV show and actually smiles when I return. There yet may be a satisfactory end to this. I explain the results and the care plan, adding that the urine test is not back yet, but when it is, they will be dismissed. The child appears to be napping. When the urine returns I am a bit surprised that a little microscopic blood was detected. That could indicate an early urine infection, as I have found nothing physically wrong with the child. Nothing at all.

Mom is still engrossed in the TV, but my radar is up. For some reason, I'm unnecessarily concerned about the trace of blood. I hate to make patient errors or miss a diagnosis, so I decide to re-examine the child. The child now appears flushed. I touch him to awaken him, and he is hot as hell. His fever has climbed to 105.8, and he is not actually sleeping. He is virtually unresponsive! What the hell happened? I look at his arm and where the tourniquet for the unnecessary blood test was placed, and I see petechiae (tiny red or purple spots) everywhere. These are little hemorrhages that when found below a tourniquet are usually meaningless, but in the face of an ill patient can mean impending disaster. There are now petechiae under his eyes and in the conjunctiva as well. OMG!! I had almost sent this kid home with my false reassurances and now must explain to Mom that everything has changed in just an hour's time. I tell her I now consider her child to be in critical condition. I feel a nightmare scenario is developing. Mom calmly takes this news in stride, which surprises me.

I do a quick lumbar puncture that reassuringly returns what looks like normal spinal fluid. In this situation, though, I waste no time pulling out the stops to treat this child for severe septic shock. I request fluid boluses, two IV antibiotics, and calls to the pediatric ICU in the children's hospital to arrange for a transfer. This little boy has no simple virus; he has life-threatening sepsis brought on by meningitis.

This type of case is rare. Such a catastrophic progression of illness also is rare, but it is typical of meningococcal sepsis. I figure in my head that this disease has a 50 percent mortality rate. Just an hour ago this child looked and acted well. When things like this happen, it shakes one's confidence in medicine and oneself. We can't cure everything, but when a small child is abruptly thrust into this much danger, it is hard to accept. I see that the child is intubated and placed on a ventilator and say my goodbyes to Mom. I offer best wishes, but I can't forget what has just transpired.

I call the ICU the next day to see how he is. The doc says holding his own and even has improved. He might be extubated and off the ventilator later that afternoon. He comments about the antibiotics and thanks me for starting them so soon. That might have saved the child's life, he says. The next day I go over to see the patient. Unbelievably, he is watching a cartoon in the ICU! Disaster averted. I say hi to him, and, of course, he doesn't remember me. His one question is, "Why am I wearing a diaper? I don't wear diapers anymore." I am so relieved and happy for him I could cry but don't. Instead, I share a laugh with the staff.

Blood, urine, and spinal fluid all grew the dreaded meningococcal bacteria. His response to care is just short of a miracle. I am so relieved I listened to my inner voice—and to a request for simple lab work. A quick blood or urine test can actually save a life, even when it seems unnecessary.

I tell myself: Always listen to Mom. She just might be right.

PC

GETTING HURT WHILE TRYING TO HELP

Dear Jack,

Do you ever wonder whether our existence is governed by something other than statistical probability? I sometimes envision the forces of good and evil locked in a tug-of-war. Sometimes good is winning, sometimes evil.

I imagined this on a Saturday morning about a year-and-a-half ago. It was still early, and the last of the night's cases were being discharged. The influx of new patients hadn't yet begun, so it was a welcome, quiet morning.

EMS then appeared with a twenty-four-year-old woman who came from the county lockup with a knee injury. She had been playing volleyball, sprained her knee, and was complaining of pain and swelling. Actually, she was yelling about her pain as they wheeled her to her ER bay. My first thought was a bit selfish. I was thinking how unfair this scenario seemed to me. I am here working the weekend shift on a beautiful spring morning, but the convicted felon doing a sixty-day stint on drug charges was out playing volleyball. It seemed so unfair, so incongruous.

Her chart was the only one on the rack, so I immediately picked it up and went to her bedside to evaluate her. Not much of a medical history other than some prior drug use, mainly opiates, along with IV drugs and the occasional crack rock. She is hepatitis B-positive, which poses a minor risk to care

48

providers. She says that she had jumped up while running forward to the net and when she came down on her knee, it popped. Then came the pain. Since the injury is just an hour ago, her knee had become quite swollen. Without taking a breath, she complained again of the pain.

Some patients appear to have a "low pain threshold." She may be one of them. Yes, her knee is injured, probably a torn cruciate ligament, but her reaction seems a bit theatric. I also consider drug-seeking behavior. This is when a patient, often with a history of drug abuse, complains loudly of pain in the hopes of extracting a prescription for opiates, or at least a single injection of one. They are a constant strain on all of us.

I pull the sheet off her legs and start my exam. Her knee is moderately swollen, about a grade three out of four effusion, so not the most severe. She is difficult to examine as she complains of pain with even light skin palpation. I realize I won't learn much more from further examination. I do suspect she has torn her anterior cruciate ligament, but this is not an emergency. I explain she will be placed in a knee immobilizer, is to use crutches, apply ice four or more times daily, and take ibuprofen. Predictably, she immediately requests hydrocodone. I explain that the preferred treatment is without hydrocodone, and with her history of drug abuse, I cannot give her that. She begins to cry. I turn and walk to the desk to complete her chart. And then she ups the ante to a loud wail, as I get ever further away from her. It's amazing that all drug users require hydrocodone and cry if they don't get it.

She moans the whole time the nurse tries to discharge her, and I start to think more about her situation. I am not attempting to be mean, and I have offered her the standard care. And the ibuprofen will provide some anti-inflammatory effect that hydrocodone won't. But I do realize ice bags four or more times per day, staying off her leg for the first couple of days, and getting ibuprofen delivered to her jail cell are all highly unlikely to happen. So, I take pity on her.

I go back and offer to drain the effusion, a procedure that will give her some added relief. "Yes, please, doctor," she says. There is some risk in doing this drainage, such as causing an infection in her knee joint, but she still wants it done. I am not that busy, and a procedure that is not strictly indicated but will offer some relief, seems like the humane course to take. I tell the ER tech to do a full five-minute scrub and set up the tray for the needle drainage as well.

When he is done, I do a second scrub because I want to be certain I don't cause an infection. I then paint the area with a disinfectant called betadine, and lay sterile drapes all around her knee. I carefully explain that there will be a little stinging when I give the local anesthetic and that she must hold still. She may yell if she likes, but please do not move. The numbing goes well, she doesn't flinch, and so I do an extra good job of infiltrating anesthetic deeply around the joint capsule where the needle will enter it. That is the most painful part of the procedure. I drain off about 150cc of bloody fluid and am now pretty certain she has torn that ligament. As I remove the needle, a painless portion of the procedure, it suddenly happens.

For some reason, she jumps unexpectedly, kicks her leg up, grabs my arm, and the needle I am removing from her skin with my right hand is pulled out toward my left hand, and the fucking needle sticks me in the index finger. She says, "I felt a pinch," even before I could ask why she jumped and grabbed my hand. The anger on my face probably had told her the question that was coming.

I immediately pull off the glove thinking maybe I wasn't really stuck. But there it was, a little dot of blood welling up on my left index finger. I went over to the wash sink and doused it in betadine soap, and scrubbed for two minutes. Then straight betadine, trying to massage it deep into the puncture. Then I add hydrogen peroxide. I know I can't really clean the depths of a puncture wound, but I gave it my damnedest. This is an IV drug abuser's blood that has been inoculated into my finger.

I am now seething. I hate this woman right now. I now have a needle stick from a known drug abuser that I didn't need, delivered during the most painful part of the procedure, the removal of the needle. Worse yet, this should not have happened at all. But her childish behavior during a humanitarian gesture on my part reminds me of the adage: No good deed goes unpunished. I am so mad I can hardly contain myself. It's not the hepatitis B I know she has that worries me as I am already immunized against it. I'm worried about something called hepatitis C, or worse yet, HIV. No effective preventive treatment is available for either at this time. I am now in the hands of fate, or something else.

I explain her discharge will be delayed as we test her for HIV. She says she is negative and was recently tested. I say fine, then we can expect a negative result. I make her wait for the test result.

While the tests do return negative, a comforting thing, there's a chance she has the AIDS virus and is in the eight-week (or so) window during which she hasn't yet developed antibodies. That would make the test falsely negative, but she is still contagious during this period. I review all this with our infectious disease specialist. He offers me his condolences but advises me to use barrier contraception for nine months and be retested periodically until then.

My patient is discharged and gone from my life, I hope. My wife and I will now worry for the better part of the coming year. I sulk at the desk for a while pondering all of this and muse about the good and evil. Is it possible there is a struggle between the two that goes on just beyond our senses? I imagine a family having fun playing on a river, grilling hot dogs, and drinking sodas and beer. Is good triumphing right then? And when one of them falls from the rope swing, landing at the water's edge and striking the back of their neck on a protruding rock, destined to be quadriplegic, has evil prevailed? Or do we live in a world governed only by probabilities, statistical variation, and standard deviations? I don't have an answer for these questions. But at that moment, I felt like evil has won.

Nine months drag by, and happily, I remain negative for both diseases. Has good prevailed?

About eighteen months after the needle stick, she is back in the ER, and I am working. She doesn't recognize me, but I do her. She is in horrible health and now has developed AIDS. Once again, the role of fate in our lives occurs to me. What if she had had the HIV virus when I was stuck? What if I had converted to HIV positive while simply trying to help relieve her pain? What if it was me now in the ER as an AIDS patient? What will become of her now?

Well Jack, I am fine, so maybe good prevailed that day after all. I hope that I am protected from other diseases to which I no doubt will be exposed. I hope that good acts win the war.

PC

ONE LUCKY DUCK

Dear Jack,

Every time I think I have seen it all, I set myself up for the next surprise. No textbook can prepare you for the bizarre cases that arrive without warning. Just your training, past experience, and common sense can guide you. And of course, keeping your cool in the face of a terrible situation. Excitement moves to panic, and as I mentioned in a previous letter, it can be contagious. Such feelings must be kept in control. I learned to keep my cool long ago with the sage advice of Samuel Shem, author of **The House of God**, a funny novel that documents the escapades of six interns. Shem says, "At a cardiac arrest, the first procedure is to take your own pulse."

The emergency physician's mantra is to follow the ABCs of keeping patients alive: Airway, Breathing, and Circulation. These are the three things we assess and address first because the absence of any of these functions can kill rapidly. A good look at the patient as they arrive is very helpful as well. You gain a gestalt of the overall situation. You get an idea of their level of alertness, their breathing mechanics, and how they move. Purposeful or combative? Or maybe they're not moving at all.

I am working my ER shift when the encoder announces yet another incoming patient. The encoder's tone and the announcement of an unconscious patient will get everyone's attention. It holds the promise of a challenge and an opportunity to do real emergency medicine. This one is sixty-year-old man who lost consciousness and is having severe respiratory distress. These cases can go either way, and I realize that if this is as bad as it sounds, the only thing standing between my patient and the grave is little ol' me. This may strike you as odd, but the truth is, I still feel like just me. Not an experienced emergency physician. Just a person. With a mission. And some training.

As we prepare a crash bed and start setting out the equipment, my mind is racing. What could be the cause? We call this "the differential diagnosis," when a range of possibilities could be causing a condition and it's up to us to narrow it down. This process can frequently point us in the right direction early in the case. It also helps me think of the unusual members of the possible diagnostic group, the so-called zebras that pop up from time to time. We learn to look for horses when we hear hoof beats, but zebras have hoofs, too. I love a zebra. For now, though, I know where to start: The ABCs. Every time. Every patient.

EMS rolls the gurney into a fully equipped crash/trauma bay. The patient is getting Bag-Valve-Mask (BVM) ventilation by the paramedic with high-flow oxygen. He is motionless. I see a rather scruffy looking male under the mask, unshaven and reeking of cigarette smoke.

The paramedic accompanying this patient is someone I know well. He is very good and talks to me as we unload the patient. Not much medical history is available, unfortunately. I am always disappointed when I can't learn more about the patients from the events leading to their arrival. The paramedic tells me the patient was found on the kitchen floor. He seemed to be getting a little bit of air as he attempted to breathe, and the oxygen helped. With the hospital close by, no attempt was made to put down a breathing tube. Fine. When possible, I prefer to do that myself anyway.

As always, I begin with A. The airway. I quickly open his mouth and it is clear of foreign material or secretions. Even before the next step though the odd way the patient is breathing immediately strikes me. Instead of expanding with each breathing attempt, his chest collapses somewhat. I do a quick pupil check before I move on, as his oxygen saturations are OK for the few seconds I spend on this. They are round, equal, perhaps a bit sluggish, but reactive. A good sign, I think. I open his mouth with suction at the ready but the pharynx is clear. B. Breathing. I listen to his chest, and, yes, there is some minimal air motion with a quiet but audible soft inspiratory whistling noise. Not a lot. But audible if you are listening carefully. I'm not sure what is causing this. His oxygen saturation is good on high flow oxygen. C. Circulation. Blood pressure is fine. Heart rate is elevated. Capillary refill is good. One of the nurses reports his blood glucose is a normal 120. I see no trauma.

For a case like this, we have a crowd of staff at the ready. Two nurses. Two ER techs. Hospital respiratory tech. Radiology techs. Often a rotating student, intern, or resident or two. And often the ER charge nurse of the day. Everyone has his or her job. They are a well-rehearsed group that knows what to do without me saying a thing.

Given his unconscious status without a definite cause, I give the orders to prepare for intubation. I must act to protect his airway, improve his breathing, and protect his lungs from aspiration. Aspiration of gastric contents can spell pneumonia and, possibly, a fatal lung injury. The respiratory tech gets the ventilator ready and the nurse starts drawing paralytic and sedative drugs. I have the laryngoscope in my hand and suction ready. I take the opportunity to more fully evaluate the airway before I paralyze him.

His jaw opens wide and I see a Class I airway, which means there's a lot of room for an easy intubation. The team is still not quite ready to insert the tube to connect to a ventilator. So, I use these precious seconds to look a little further. I insert the laryngoscope carefully deeper into the hypopharynx to take a look around. OMG! I see what looks like a huge carcinoma in his lower airway blocking airflow. It is gray-brown and irregular in shape. It looks both fungating and polypoid, a tumor marked by breaks and dead tissue.

I remove the scope and we continue to support him while I think a minute before we administer the drugs that will paralyze him. I am concerned I may not be able to intubate him after he is paralyzed. I also have a number of other concerns. This tumor looks necrotic. Dying tissue. I suspect it began to accumulate water (become edematous) and became engorged to the point of blocking his airway. If I try to displace it by moving the endotracheal tube down past the tumor, it may start bleeding and he will drown in his own blood. It looks very easy to crumble, I think. Perhaps I should just do a cricothyrotomy, which involves cutting into the neck, below the tumor, to create an airway. In this fashion I can establish the airway without causing a bleeding mess. I haven't done one in a while, but it will be a challenge, which I enjoy. The staff is always primed for life-saving heroics. I'm feeling pumped until the thought of *primum non nocere* suddenly slows me down. First, do no harm. I need to think a bit more. I do not want to harm my patient, but I do need to address his breathing problem quickly. I order the cricothyrotomy tray to be set up. The staff is excited. "Doc's gonna cric this guy," I hear the ER tech call out. Maybe, I think, but not quite yet. I need another look. I fully realize time is of the essence, but the decisions I make right now are critical.

I take the scope in for another look. I realize there is no need to paralyze him; he is completely unresponsive. No motion. No gagging. Nothing. I slowly advance the scope and I get to the obstructing tumor. Carcinoma of the larynx from years of smoking, I presume. And then I notice something odd.

I see what looks like an anise seed stuck to the surface of the cancerous growth. My mind skips ahead. The tumor is irregular and probably just has some recently consumed food stuck there. And then I notice two more such seeds. And what looks like red pepper flakes! And I can differentiate little chunks of fat mixed with the tumor. What the hell am I looking at?

This tumor looks oddly familiar. I'm half Sicilian and proud of it. I grew up eating hot Italian sausage in deep red Sicilian sauce with ravioli on Christmas Eve. Grilled sausage on New Year's Eve. Baked sausage. Fried sausage. I love them all. And my background comes to my assistance just when I need it most. I suddenly realize I am looking at the surface of a damn Italian hot sausage! Not a tumor at all. I ask for the Magill forceps and they appear in my hands. I have a good team. No delay, the right drawer opened the first time. I am immediately comforted to have good, capable people around me.

Everyone watches in quiet amazement. I haven't said anything more about the cancerous growth but am busy doing something with the Magills in his throat. I carefully grasp the sausage with the forceps and gently attempt to extract it. It gives way immediately and I pull out a single hunk of what is probably half an entire sausage. In a theatrical moment, I drop it on the patient's chest along with the forceps. The staff reaction is the same as mine. Incredulous. My friend, the paramedic, is standing at the bedside with his mouth wide open. Nobody can believe what has just happened. Including me. I suction the airway. And we briefly bag-ventilate the patient again.

His eyes open. He focuses on me. Suddenly, he is wide awake. And then he utters words I can't believe. In a slightly hoarse voice he calmly says, "Thank you, doctor." I allow myself a big tension-breaking laugh. We have gone from a major emergency to this guy, matter-of-factly, offering a thank you just minutes later. By now, I've been around the proverbial block, but this is surreal. We let him rest a bit. I go back to talk with him. He says he heard everything that was going on since he choked on the sausage and collapsed. He was paralyzed with fear when he struggled to breathe and realized he couldn't. So, he just lay absolutely still from the time he went down on the kitchen floor, trying to gently take each breath, all the while listening to the events around him. That had to take incredible self-control.

His chest X-ray returns and looks normal. His blood gas measurements, drawn when he first arrived, return with a CO_2 over a hundred and a satisfactory oxygen concentration. A mild acidosis is obvious as well. As the carbon dioxide built up in his system because of his nearly completely blocked airway, he became sedated by it. Acute CO_2 elevations do this to the brain. This effect may, in fact, have saved his life and prevented him from sucking the sausage down tight into his larynx and causing his death.

Most adult choking events involve a large chunk of meat. I recall reading an article that said the average chunk in such fatal episodes is about half the size of a cigarette pack. Typically, alcohol is involved. The combination of a mildly inebriated brain, a tasty meal, and an over-zealous appetite can and does sometimes kill.

I observe him for a couple of hours. He calmly watches the events transpiring in our busy ER. It is one huge room with beds positioned all around a large workstation. He is intently watching the happenings from his front row seat.

Later, I discharge him home. "Chew your food," I say. I don't have much more than that to offer. I think I have heard this advice myself as a child. Perhaps a thousand times. I was always in a hurry to get back to the street baseball game, touch football on the blacktop, or hide-and-seek. He says thank you again and walks out of our lives. One. Lucky. Duck.

As I mentioned, sometimes I think I have seen it all. I am always proven wrong. Cases like this are very satisfying. A good save. A good challenge. And a patient who walks away unscathed by me or the health care system. Primum non nocere. I managed to do that today.

With that thought, I celebrate alone. My patient was lucky, and so was I. Everyone else has moved on to doing what they do so well. Saving lives.

PC

A MASS CASUALTY

Dear Jack,

The power of the mind always surprises me. What gets me is how we can believe almost anything, if we try hard enough. And also that, no matter how hard we try, sometimes, we can't stop believing other things. Things that aren't true.

Panic has a way of clouding our thinking. It's what most people feel when they are stressed, perceive a grave threat, or think their life is in danger. Without a conscious thought, panic informs you to run. Get away while you can. You are going to die. Often, though, if you just give it a little time and more thought, you realize the situation may not be as dire as it seems. But in the moment, just when you need your brain to work at full power, it seems to fail you.

You see, the area of the brain called the amygdala makes fast decisions based on limited information, going into high gear shouting, "Danger! Danger, Will Robinson!" The amygdala gets flooded with adrenalin. That response, that I call the Amygdala Hijack had a purpose as we evolved. Imagine you're on the African plain in high grass when you see a patch of tawny fur moving toward you. Your amygdala yells, "Shit! A lion!" Adrenalin pumps through your veins, and off you run. Your amygdala's fight-or-flight response may have saved your life. Now, before you credit or blame the amygdala for everything, the prefrontal cortex may weigh in. It can override the amygdala's hasty conclusions. This area says, "Wait a second, let's think about this." The tawny patch is not charging. It may not be a threat. It may in fact be an antelope. And I have a spear. This may be a good meal. And, lo and behold, the antelope appears, looks the other way, and bingo. Dinner for twenty. So, both areas have an evolutionary purpose. But that amygdala is what leads to panic. And panic, Jack, can be contagious.

It's about mid-morning on an average shift when the encoder calls out an alert to the ER. Firefighters are at the scene of a possible toxic gas exposure. A mother and child are reporting difficulty breathing, and firefighters detect an odd chemical odor in the house. This could be interesting, I think. I have had a special interest in toxicology and poisons since childhood. In medical school, I did a lot of extra reading on the subject.

I quickly survey the ER and I have three monitored beds open. Perfect, I think, one more than I need. Bring 'em on.

My own amygdala usually remains asleep or has been trained to keep its panicky mouth shut. Very useful for an ER doc. There are a few concerned questions from the staff about bringing patients exposed to a toxin into the area. The risk is that we will all become poisoned. I reassure them. I will first check the patients outside and evaluate the situation. A toxic gas is highly unlikely to be brought into the ER anyway, and we can have the fire department and EMS decontaminate the patients before they come in. I'm convinced keeping their amygdalas quiet should be my goal. I don't need a panicked staff.

I have a respiratory tech paged to come STAT, as we may need immediate ventilator support and arterial blood gas analysis. That's all the prep we need for the moment. There are only two hazmat suits in the hospital, anyway, so I can forget about getting them out for me and my staff. They can be a great safety blanket in such situations, but bringing them out and suiting up right now will just heighten everyone's worries. I leave them in whatever storage room they live in.

Over the next fifteen minutes, the encoder screams out again and again. More victims are falling. Two firefighters, one police officer, and another child have lost consciousness and are on the floor. I can hear rising panic in the voice on the radio. My own amygdala threatens to join the crowd, but in times like this, I know keeping my own calm is essential. I have patients moved to hallway beds, more rooms opened, two more respiratory techs paged, and a radiology tech standing by in the ER. A quick chest X-ray might help immensely with making a diagnosis.

And then it happens. The shit truly seems to be hitting the fan as I now have ten patients enroute with difficulty breathing and altered consciousness. You can feel the adrenalin surging throughout the ER. I toy with calling a mass-casualty alert. I decide to hold off. I am not alone in the ER today and have a resident or two to help me. One more patient, though, and I am pulling the ripcord and calling a hospital-wide alert. I have three more ventilators quickly brought into the ER and lab staff waiting as well. This whole situation will test everything I have learned over the past several years. Everything.

And then they start rolling in. Still only ten casualties. The fire department is reporting finding nothing. None of the few toxins they can test for on the scene is showing any presence. No carbon monoxide. No leaking gas pipes. Hmmmm, I wonder. Just what is going on?

I check the first patients outside as thoroughly as I can. All are awake, with rapid respirations, eyes wide open, and pupils dilated. Heart rates are in the 120's or so. Airways are clear, and they have good air motion in their lungs. No weird odors. I let them come into the ER, one by one, to beds fitted with cardiac monitors. I caution staff to wear gloves, remove and bag all clothing, then take it outside.

Multiple labs are ordered on everyone, including blood gas analysis, EKG's, and chest X-rays. A couple of patients also get a few milligrams of Valium intravenously to calm them down. Every patient looks exactly the same clinically. I reassure them all that we will take good care of them. Relax, I say. You are in a good place.

And now my prefrontal cortex kicks in, and I take time to think. And think some more. And nothing makes sense. Everyone is getting better, calming down. Their amygdalas have quieted down. I am starting to consider that high on the differential diagnosis list is "nothing wrong." No toxin present.

I now have time to really talk with the hazardous substances fire department staff from the scene. I learn that the gas was coming from the washroom area of the house. From a bucket. A firefighter smelled chlorine and a rotten odor. I speculate about hydrogen sulfide, which can be deadly if inhaled even in low concentrations. But was there enough to hurt anyone? I doubt it.

Every piece of lab work, X-rays, and EKGs appear in a pile on my desk as I go from patient to patient, rechecking, reassuring, and watching everything return to normal. All heart rates are normal. The staff is still not performing as usual and I have to sort through the paper and separate the documents into piles for each patient. Every single test on every single patient is normal. Every EKG and X-ray is normal. I am sure glad I didn't pull that mass-casualty alert. The new guy calling an unnecessary alert would make me look like an idiot. I'd probably be permanently dropped from the ER work schedule, as well.

The staff keeps asking what I think. I begin to speak openly with them about mass panic and hyperventilation. I can find nothing wrong with anybody. I get the fire department on the radio and ask for the toxic bucket to be brought to the hospital so I can examine it. I need to see for myself before I call bullshit. I sure don't want to make a mistake and have someone die. Primum non nocere. They are hesitant as they have seen their comrades fall, but I assure them everyone is fine now. Just bring me the bucket, I say.

They bring it to the parking lot about a hundred yards from the ER entrance. They ask if I want a hazmat suit, and I answer no. Before they can stop me, I trot out to the offending bucket. It smells of bleach and a separate rotten odor. For a moment, I start to wonder again about hydrogen sulfide but quickly dismiss it. It's a rapidly acting toxin that I would have seen some clinical or lab evidence for, and my patients' symptoms would not have resolved so quickly and completely once they were in the hospital. I find a stick and stir the bucket. I lift out a couple of baby poop soiled diapers. I want to laugh. What I have here is only a diaper bucket. Good souls who are saving the landfill and a few bucks doing dirty diapers the old way. Nice.

I quickly conclude I now have a substantial public relations problem. The news media is outside. They've heard the chatter on their police and fire radios. Just how am I going to tell this group of professionals and the family they simply panicked? Mass hyperventilation all brought on by a bucket of dirty diapers! As I said, panic is contagious.

I do my best with explanations. I even stretch the truth and offer that there may have been some actual minor chlorine exposure. I know it's bullshit, but I'm trying to help the emergency responders save face. They'd endure weeks of ridicule and maybe even question their own self-confidence if word got out that they simply panicked over a little poop. That would not be good.

I'm only partly successful in my endeavor. Everyone goes home and back to work. But for months, every time I see EMS I feel like they are giving me the stink eye. There's the doctor who called us all crazy. Oh well, I sympathize and did my best.

The episode strengthens my already strong belief that when I see panic in the eyes of my staff, I must remain calm. Even nonchalant. Because calm is also contagious. And I want them to catch it from me.

PC

THINGS CAN CHANGE IN MINUTES

Dear Jack,

As in life, things change, often unpredictably. So it goes in medicine. One day you are just fine and the next day something changes your life. You wake up with chest pain, cough up blood, or have severe stomach pain. And you soon learn a medical catastrophe is in progress, and it may even kill you. Or you could have an accident or be the victim of a crime. Regardless, the thing that changes everything is a "when" event, not an "if" event. "It" happens to all of us.

Today, change is in store for this young man. Unpredictable change. Something I can guarantee he never once worried about.

It is mid-morning and I watch my patient being wheeled into a suture bed on a gurney by EMS. He appears to be in his mid-twenties, is awake and alert, and even joking with the paramedics. I wonder silently why he is arriving by ambulance as all I can see is a small bandage wrapped around his head. Not even any visible blood. "Just a scalp lac, doc," I hear the paramedic call out as I walk over. And with that they pack up their gear and head out to the next call.

My patient tells me he was walking under the bridge that spans a hiking trail near our lake downtown. Someone had thrown or dropped a rock at him, apparently. All he can tell me is he felt it hit on the side of the head and then there was blood. A lot of it. And he called for help on his cellphone.

Scalp lacerations are particularly frightening for patients as they tend to bleed profusely. The bleeding is not always related to the seriousness of the wound; rather, it can simply be the result of a lot of blood vessels in the scalp. Scary no doubt, but usually easily stopped with a simple bandage and a little firm hand pressure.

I go through my history and exam and don't find much to be concerned about. A two-inch laceration to the side of his head that looks like a simple sewing job. There was no loss of consciousness and I find no red flags on exam. But I am a cautious sort and such an impact over a small area of the skull can cause a depressed skull fracture. That wound might yet harbor a surprise. I know I may be able to simply look at his skull through the wound as I sew it up, and see a fracture if it is there. I also know sometimes you can't see a fracture, so, rather than waste time, I order a CT brain scan. It will give me definitive answers without delay, and let me know what I am dealing with. I don't like to go home worrying about patients, and the only way I have found to prevent that is to be thorough. Life is full of surprises in the ER. And things can change, including a perception that an injury is no big deal.

Perhaps thirty minutes pass and I see him being rolled back into the ER bed. It is all set up for a little suturing. The radiology tech offers that it must have been a busy night for this guy because he is now napping. I'll go over and wake him in a few minutes and get that sewing job done.

I saunter over to the bedside and he sure seems to be sleeping soundly. For a second I regret having to wake him from his nap. I shake his shoulder gently, but he doesn't easily awaken. He seems groggy now and a little confused. This is not the patient I saw just thirty minutes ago. I get him sitting up and walk over to see if the CT scan is done yet. You see, the scanner takes all of the images very quickly, but it takes a few minutes for the computer to turn all of that data into a reconstructed picture of his brain.

I am shocked when I see his images. Things have changed alright, and in a bad way. I see the telltale accumulation of white on the scan, just under where the laceration is. This white is blood in the area surrounding his brain and it has the feared lens shape of what's called an epidural hematoma. This is a life-threatening and potentially rapidly progressing emergency. I also see a depressed fragment of bone pressing into the surface of his brain. Damn, I am thinking, glad to have ordered this CT scan. I return to the bed to let him know just how things have changed.

Holy fucking crap, in the five minutes it took to look at the CT scan, he has gone from slightly groggy to comatose! I yell out for help, and we move him into the trauma bay. One pupil is now dilated, or blown as we say, indicating severe pressure building on his brain. When I stimulate him, I now find his response is what we call "posturing." An extension and inward rotation of his arms, that like the blown pupil, signals a brain that is dying from excess intracranial pressure. I have the clerk page the neurosurgeon STAT. Respiratory therapy STAT. Drugs for sedation and then a drug to cause paralysis as I prepare him for the intubation. Happily, it's easy to do, and he is on the ventilator. We will try to keep the carbon dioxide in his blood at just slightly below normal, as an excess will increase the pressure on the brain even more. I order mannitol, a drug that will dehydrate him somewhat. By removing a little of his blood volume and a little water from his brain, the drug will decrease the pressure on his brain and buy time for emergency surgery. My neurosurgeon arrives quickly as he was already in the hospital. Off they go into surgery. Time is crucial for a good outcome, so every minute matters.

I am now thankful my patient called EMS for help and didn't just decide to walk home. Maybe check in the mirror to see if he even needed to see a doctor. Had he taken this route, he would have been found dead later in the day. Jeez. I make a mental note to go and see him tomorrow during my next shift. I want to see how he fared and let him know what a life-saving decision he made to call for help.

My next shift is busy, and I simply don't have time to check him. Then, I am off for a couple days. I call my neurosurgeon friend and learn the patient has done well and has been discharged to his home. Disaster averted.

As I said, things change. Often, I find a life has gone from its normal daily routine to a possibly fatal problem. All in the blink of an eye. I dread "my day" but try to avoid thinking about it too much. I have also found it will most likely be from something I never saw coming, something I never once worried about. So why worry? Worry is mostly wasted energy, preventing you from enjoying all of your good days. I want to enjoy all of my good days. Unless I am one of the lucky ones who goes to bed one night and dies while sleeping, I, too, will have a surprise one day that changes everything.

And that is life and death in the ER. It's all about surprises and the things that change for everyone.

PC

A NEAR-DEATH EXPERIENCE

Dear Jack,

I'm in my hospital's trauma rooms, what we call the crash area of the ER today. It started like most others and picked up steam around 11 a.m. More ambulances and gurneys are coming and going. Incessant overhead pages as nurses and doctors hunt for each other. It's noisy, but not as bad as a weekend night. Some patients are frightened, but most are calm and quiet. One we had today is different.

You could hear him from the ambulance entrance as he was wheeled on a gurney down the back hallway, with EMS and a police escort in tow. As he gets closer, I hear him cursing loudly and being a real jackass. As he is wheeled into crash room six, I am thinking this thirty-five-year-old juvenile is either drunk or drugged, and it isn't even noon. Jeez. I see him spitting on the floor and still cursing as the staff tries to start an IV. He's clearly a dyed-in-the-wool jerk. I look up at the heart monitor though and am immediately concerned.

We don't use the regular monitor except for heart rate and rhythm tracking. We rely on a regular EKG for most of the rest. But on this monitor, I can see what we call tombstones. A section of the EKG tracing that is elevated above the baseline and indicates a heart attack in progress. We get the

EKG attached despite his persistent belligerence. Yes, an acute anterior wall myocardial infarction is well underway. My suspicion is confirmed.

I figure he is on cocaine, which has caused his heart to rebel. He denies everything except that he feels a tremendous pressure in his chest. It won't go away. Started an hour ago. I begin entering our protocol orders for an acute MI. I also order a little Valium IV. This sedative will help block the effects of the presumed cocaine. If nothing else, it should cool him down and make him a little more tractable. I also page the cardiologist STAT.

The cardiologist calls back quickly, and I give him the rundown. I explain that despite the patient's age, he appears to have a blocked left main artery supplying the heart muscle. I ask whether we should start the man on thrombolytics, the clot-buster drugs. Not yet, the cardiologist responds. I can tell from his tone he is not even convinced this is a legitimate heart attack. "Should I start prepping him for a cardiac stent then?" I ask. He will have to take the patient to the cardiac catheterization room, what we call the cath lab, to open the artery with a stent. These are small tubes inserted directly into the clogged artery to allow the blood to flow again. Wait, the cardiologist says again. He is in the hospital and will be down in less than five minutes. He wants to see this one for himself.

He is close so, I don't mind waiting, although I continue to be amazed when other doctors who have not even seen the patient, much less the EKG, think they could possibly be better informed than I am. We have a saying, "Time is muscle." The longer we wait before acting, the less heart muscle we can save.

I go ahead with the other treatments: aspirin, some intravenous nitrates. I hold off on the heart-relaxing beta-blocker because it can make things worse if we're dealing with a cocaine overdose. A lot worse, actually, causing his blood pressure to skyrocket. Not what you want during a heart attack. So, for now, we give him a little morphine.

The cardiologist arrives and immediately agrees. This is the type of heart attack we call "the widow maker." The entire anterior wall of his heart is screaming for oxygen and dying as the clock ticks. The cardiologist dashes across the hall to check out the cath lab suites to see how soon we can get this guy back for an emergency stent. I ask the nurses to pull the crash cart into the room as my hackles are up. I have a feeling it's going to get worse. Over the years, I have learned to listen to my internal radar. When it goes off, I pay attention.

And then it happens. Right then and there. I hear a nurse yell from his room as the monitor alarms sound loudly. He has just had a cardiac arrest. I am there in seconds, and he is already a hideous blue color. It amazes me how some patients turn so obviously blue so dang fast. The monitor shows ventricular fibrillation. A heart that is simply quivering and no longer pumping blood. My ER staff is good. I don't need to yell to start CPR because this staff is already doing it. They also have placed defib pads on the patient's chest when I had them bring over the crash cart. That is the kind of attention to detail that saves lives. Lots of activity and only a minute has gone by. I charge up the defibrillator and shout, "Clear!" to be heard over the room noise. The staff falls away from the patient. If they don't step back, they could be shocked as well. His body gives the typical convulsive jolt, but his heartbeat remains chaotic. We restart CPR and I charge the defibrillator again at a higher energy level. I yell again, and then a shock. He gives the convulsive jerk, and, voila, his heart is beating again. I order CPR for one more minute because a heart that has been just quivering abnormally for so long won't immediately start pumping blood with the usual force. His pulse returns and we stop CPR. What happens next though is where the story actually gets interesting.

Often with a very brief cardiac arrest, the patient will wake up almost immediately. They're usually confused, a bit agitated, or even combative. Most of the time, with some reassurance that everything is OK, they settle down. He, however, is immediately wide-awake. Just like it never happened.

I'm not looking forward to his nasty behavior returning, but, oddly, he is as calm as a nun. Something has changed. He just stares at me. He asks me, "Sir, what just happened?" I am shocked. Sir?! Out of this guy's trash mouth?

The cath lab won't be free for another twenty minutes, so we start the necessary drugs to prep him for an intracardiac stent. Suddenly, I am alone with him in the room. He says, "Doc, tell me again. What happened to me?" I explain again that his heart temporarily stopped but that things are under control now. He persists. "So, I was dead for a while, right?" My interest is piqued. I say, "Yes, more or less." He is now as polite as an English gentleman. I am interested in near-death experiences, although I don't know what they mean. And then, he starts talking again, and the hairs on my arms stand up, and a cold chill literally sweeps over me.

He says he went to heaven and stood before God. He explains all that he saw. First were the bright lights often reported with near-death experiences. He says he could hear church organ music. After a sensation of rushing upwards he says he stood directly before God. Right before God, he insists. The look on his face was pure awe. God told him he needed to change his life. No more drugs, no more being an asshole. He was being granted a second chance. And there we were together. At the start of his new life, his second chance. He is clearly shaken and has been deeply moved by this experience.

It was surreal to hear those words from his mouth. Science attempts to explain near-death experiences as the misfiring of a dying brain. We hallucinate right before the brain goes silent forever. But I have to wonder. What really happened today? Did he see God? I still have cold chills as he leaves for the cath lab. I love my job today.

By the way, his drug screen turned out to be negative for everything. No cocaine. Just the bad luck and bad genes that lead to a heart attack at thirty-five. I wonder what he will do with his second chance. Will he really change?

"Faith is taking the first step even when you don't see the whole staircase."

Martin Luther King

PC

I'M SO SORRY

Dear Jack,

I was having a routine morning, working in what we call the ER's treatment area. This space takes care of mostly ambulatory patients, those with less-serious medical problems. A few ambulances bring them in with minor trauma, or with stable but acute medical problems. Not much of a chance of seeing anything really notable. But once in a while, a patient triaged here gives me pause, like a medical surprise package waiting behind a closed door. And most often, not a welcome one. Today turned into one of those days.

It is closing in on lunchtime. We are busy but not out of control. I hear a chart drop into the rack, turn around, and get up to retrieve it. A twenty-four-year-old man woke up with a swollen left arm. Interesting, perhaps. Probably some minor trauma, a strain, a contusion, or maybe he slept on it wrong. Probably nothing of consequence. Even at this stage of practicing medicine, I can still have naïve thoughts.

I go to a small side hall we have especially for patients with minor medical problems. It's aptly called Minor Care. As I walk in, my patient is sitting comfortably in a chair. Not on the bed where I usually find patients. He's a bit wary of being around doctors and not quite ready to admit to himself that he is a patient today. He is in no distress and tells me he woke up with his arm swollen. It's never happened before, and he can't remember any arm bump or other trauma that might have caused this. "Just a swollen arm, doc," is all he offers. Already, I don't like the feeling of foreboding this case is causing me.

It's true this complaint could turn out to be a minor one, just as he expects. Maybe he was drinking last night and just happened to sleep on this arm all night. Maybe. It can also be the first sign of a blood clot in his arm. Unusual, for sure, but they do happen in the upper extremities, even though the legs are more common. Other less savory causes also cross my worried mind.

I examine him unusually thoroughly. Touch and look at every area of him. I can see a little growing anxiety in his eyes as I check his neck, armpits, and groin for any lumps or swelling. I find nothing. I do notice, though, that his face seems slightly puffy. It's only slightly noticeable, but his cheeks and the area around his eyes appear a bit too full. I ask him if he has noticed this and he says, "Well maybe a little, but I slept for ten hours last night and got up late. My problem is my arm." Good enough, I think. No need to alarm him unnecessarily. But I am not so sure this will turn out to be a big nothing and that all he did was sleep on his arm all night, maybe after a night of chugging beers with his friends.

I explain we will need a few tests and some X-rays. He says he's fine with that, and I go back to the chart room to think a bit. I also enter orders into the computer.

The usual basic labs, for sure, a blood count, metabolic panel and blood clotting studies A special test called a D-dimer, as well. This test gives us clues to the presence of blood clots. In a low-risk patient, a negative test virtually guarantees no clot. I consider my imaging options. Probably not plain X-rays of the arm; they will tell me nothing I want to know. Most of the time, a plain X-ray is used to rule out fractures or certain types of foreign bodies. I know his arm isn't broken. I keep thinking about that puffy face. Only slightly puffy, but it continues to worry me. As I consider this, I question myself, am I just going overboard here? Being too cautious? But I order the CT scan of his chest and neck, with contrast. My radar tells me to be extra thorough here. But I have a nagging worry in the back of my brain. A little voice I have learned to listen to saying, "Be careful here. Too easy to make a mistake." When that little voice is calling out, I have learned to listen.

It's now time for lunch, so, I go back and explain what the plan of care is. I warn him this will take a while. Hospital rules require I check his kidney function before he receives the iodine contrast. His kidneys must be working well enough to eliminate the contrast after the scan without harm. I tell myself it's unnecessary to test the kidney function in a healthy young man, but there's that nagging voice in my head that also says: First, do no harm. So, I'll wait for the kidney function test. I walk down to the lunchroom, and see which of my friends I can eat with and discuss the news, politics, or whatever.

When I return, I discover he has already been taken to the scanner. Great, I think. Soon, I will have the answers I need, and he can return to his normal life.

Fifteen or twenty minutes later, I notice his images are up on the computer. No interpretation yet from the radiologist, but I am comfortable taking a look. As I review the images one by one, my stomach sours. It's not really grief I am feeling, rather sorrow. I can see within the center of his chest a mass. A rather large mass. What is causing his arm to swell is this mass is pressing on his superior vena cava, the large blood vessel that returns blood from the upper body to the heart. Because it is being compressed by the mass, blood cannot return normally. This has resulted in his arm and face swelling. I see nothing that looks like a blood clot. I scroll up to the study of his neck and feel even worse. The raised spirits I had from a good lunchtime conversation with my peers are dashed. I see what appear to be enlarged lymph nodes in his neck, even though I felt none on exam. I am relieved I chose to be thorough and careful, but I am saddened by these discoveries.

Most likely, this mass is a lymphoma, a cancer most prevalent in the young and those over sixty-five. How do I tell this young man he needs to be admitted for a work-up and a biopsy? Just the words, "A biopsy is necessary," is enough to chill the blood of many patients. I happen to know that from personal experience.

While in medical school, I noticed a small growth under my tongue one morning. Seemingly out of nowhere. I looked in the mirror and this ugly little growth had popped up where nothing should be. I went to the doctor the next day, and I heard him say, "We need a biopsy." And yes, cold chills went through me. Is this how I'll meet my end, I wondered? Probably nothing, the doc said, but it could be abnormal. Just a biopsy. Turned out to be nothing in the end. But that word just stuck in my mind for days until the results returned. I know in my heart this young man's problem will not be nothing.

How do I go back and explain the results to him? I am daunted and imagine what I might say to him. How do I explain that in a moment his life has changed? That his problem, that swollen arm, could actually be fatal or at least require grueling chemotherapy and radiation. Maybe surgery. The lymph nodes in the neck mean that, if it is lymphoma, it is already at least Stage II, a more advanced form of the disease. How do I explain that I understand yesterday he played softball with friends in the afternoon, maybe tried to charm that cute short fielder, then went out for pizza and beer, and today he has cancer. Oh my God. I dread this conversation. It's one that is hard enough with elderly patients. With someone so young, it is much more difficult, trying, and sad.

I return to his room, and although I have done my best to conceal my concerns, it is obvious I have not. I can see the growing alarm in his eyes as I walk into the room. I explain the findings and various possibilities. I include some less frightening possibilities, even though I am sure these results are actually very bad news. I have to be fair and truthful with him, but it is not in me to remove every ounce of hope.

I arrange his admission, call for a consultation with an internist and oncologist, and say my goodbyes. I wish him well. I reassure him: Even if it is a major problem like lymphoma, it is treatable. Even curable. But this young man's life has changed today. He went to bed just fine and woke up with cancer. Jeez. The arrows life throws at us are unpredictable. Most are just a nuisance, but this one is a body slam. Death at a young age is a very real possibility.

As I wait to talk to my consultants, I wonder how he will tell his parents. I simply can't imagine receiving such a call from my daughter. My feelings would be tantamount to horror. I wish no parent should have to see their child die. Sometimes, they do, though. This is a part of the job I hate the most. Giving bad news.

I only follow his course on the computer for a few days. The biopsy confirms lymphoma. Happily, it's one of the more treatable types.

I simply can't look further and follow him to the end, even if it ends well. I want that happy ending but fear what may happen. I have a daughter his age. What would I do if this were her?

I'm sorry. So sorry.

PC

WE ALL HAVE LIMITS

Dear Jack,

You simply have to know your limitations. Dirty Harry got that one right. Our prime directive is to first, do no harm, and when you stretch your limits of clinical practice beyond your training, somebody is going to suffer for it.

It's still a quiet Saturday morning as I watch the triage nurse walk a boy back to a treatment bed. He is perhaps thirteen or fourteen and is holding a gauze bandage to the side of his head. He and a friend had been goofing around in the garage when he was accidentally struck with a golf club. It's a seemingly benign scalp laceration except that I know a skull fracture is possible, particularly when the force of impact is focused on such a small area. Like with the end of a hammer, or, well, a golf club.

As the nurse walks him back to triage I ask, "A simple scalp lac?" She answers yes and adds that his private doctor is coming to see him. I grunt approval, though I would really like something to do. I'm rarely bored at work, but the ER is unusually quiet today.

It's rare for a patient's private doctor to come in and deliver personal care. Likely, the child is a friend of the doctor's family or a neighbor. There was a time when patients expected this kind of care, but today is the day of Emergency Medicine, its own specialty. An ER doctor is "very wide clinically," as we are trained to care for the first few hours of almost anything.

The specialist, on the other hand, is very narrow and knows a lot about his specialty but almost nothing about all of the other problems that come into the ER. I discover this doctor is a friend I have known for years, and if he wants to sew this laceration up, I have no complaints. I ask the tech to go ahead and set up a suture tray.

His doctor, a specialist, arrives only a few minutes later, no doubt planning on a quick hello, placing a few stitches, and then heading back to the weekend he had planned.

I fiddle around at our charting station as nothing is going on this early on a weekend morning. All of last night's traumas, drunks, and admissions to the hospital have been cleared out. As I sip my coffee, I watch my friend. Clearly out of his element, he probably hasn't done much minor surgery in years. He's clumsily fiddling with the suture tray, while an ER tech helps adjust the light and provide irrigating solution. Things seem to be moving along slowly. I wander to the doctor's lounge to grab a piece of fruit for my breakfast.

When I return, my friend is still busily futzing around with this scalp laceration. Forceps in hand, probing, looking, trimming the edges of the wound and whatever else he thinks needs to be done. This goes on for a seemingly interminable time. He looks over at me a couple of times, so, I decide to walk over and see if he needs anything.

We say our hellos and I look down at the wound, now nicely prepared with small surgical drapes. I am horrified. Inside my head I scream, "What the hell do you think you are doing?!"

Inside the wound and grasped in the forceps he is using is clearly a piece of this kid's brain! I gently pull his hand away from the wound, and he gives me a questioning but slightly irritated look. I touch him on the shoulder and whisper, "Can we talk for a minute?" Now, he simply looks puzzled, but he knows me and understands I am not going to interrupt him over nothing. I lead him several feet away and tell him bluntly that what he has been fiddling with is his patient's brain. That this is an open, depressed skull fracture and that funny looking shit that has puzzled him and that he has been picking away at is brain matter. He pales visibly, appears shaken, but does not look me in the eye. He asks if I can take it from here, and I say, of course. He pulls off his surgical gloves, drops them in the waste can, and simply walks out of the ER.

I look at the wound a little more closely, perform a neurologic exam, order a CT scan, lab work, an IV and some antibiotics. And, of course, I immediately call the neurosurgeon. I explain the change of plan to the parents and then wait for the next patient. To meddle further in this case is pointless, perhaps dangerous, and I know my limitations. Had the wound been simply closed, the outcome could have been disastrous. The CT showed an open depressed skull fracture and some minor brain hemorrhage. A close call and possibly a tragedy avoided.

I feel badly for my friend and am wondering just what he is thinking as he drives home. I hope he's hit by a realization of his limitations, just as I was when I called the neurosurgeon. We all have limits. As a clinically narrow specialist, my friend was out of his element in trying to fix this wound. That lesson has undoubtedly sunk home. I will still depend upon him for more complex medical illness, as he is a good specialist. However, acute trauma is out of his realm.

Failing to realize our limitations is a setup for doing real harm. We have to keep it humble. We must remember to do no harm.

PC

I'M NOT THE CAPTAIN, JUST ON THE CREW

Dear Jack,

I am in the crash area of the ER, working the ten-hour shift I like least, 9 p.m. to 7 a.m. It is usually exhausting. The body simply does not want to be up all night, no matter what. And because we only work two or three of these in a row, you never have a chance to adjust. I don't know who thought up these schedules. When I try to ask the older doctors about them, they just laugh and say, "Can't you take it, boy? When I was your age, I carried my sister to school uphill through the snow and back again." Right, the good old days of iron men and wooden ships must have been quite grand. Sorry I missed them. Nights can leave you physically sore all over, almost like you have been beaten with a stick.

The nighttime patient population, especially on weekend nights, is unique. The strangest of the strange don't come out until around 2 a.m. I don't know if they can't sleep or just know how strange they will seem in the broad daylight. Do they think the night protects them? I think of them as the night crawlers. Their arrival frequently means a psych consult is in the offing. Psychiatrists are often the least helpful to the ER of any consultants I encounter. For the most part, they are simply unavailable to the patients who have no health insurance or only have publicly funded coverage, like Medicaid. The patient may get a psychiatric social worker. The only time

I actually talk with a psychiatrist for a Medicaid or unfunded patient is if I am trying to admit the person to the state hospital. And then it is usually a two- to three-hour wait to speak with one directly. Otherwise, they are simply not available for phone consultation or management suggestions. The patient care could be so much better with a little more care and attention from the psychiatrist.

In the ten-bed crash unit, I tend to the sickest and most traumatically injured people. We get heart attacks, serious drug overdoses, patients in shock, and lots of car wrecks. Life-and-death events. I feel it is where we make the most difference in medical outcomes. A few quick steps and simple maneuvers can stabilize a patient for a few hours, allowing time for emergency surgery or medicines to take effect. By the same token, a misstep or having too little time to act can be deadly. Overall, it can be very satisfying, if not unnerving at times.

About 1 a.m. we get a call from the medics bringing us a GSW, or gunshot wound, to the abdomen. That's usually a pretty straightforward case. Just a matter of getting the surgeon in and deciding how fast we'll need to get the patient into the operating room. We aren't always in a rush even with a GSW. It frequently takes a surprisingly long time to die. Forget about what you have seen on TV: Guy is shot in the stomach and then collapses dead. That's rare.

Anyway, this time we will be in a hurry. The patient's blood pressure is only eighty and his heart rate 160! This usually means that we can expect the patient to be bleeding to death. He finally arrives, a young black man in his late-twenties who looks tough and says he's been smoking crack most of the day. Now, he is begging for his life. Between him pleading, "Please save me, doc," he wants us to call his mother, of all things. The incongruity of it strikes me. Given his unstable condition there is no time to call his mother right then.

The trauma surgeon and I confer over his EKG, which shows us he is in an abnormal cardiac rhythm called SVT, or supraventricular tachycardia. SVT is a dangerously fast heartbeat that occurs when the usual electric system of the heart short circuits. This would seem to make sense as an explanation for at least part of his shock condition and crack can cause this rhythm disturbance. Anesthesia doesn't want to take him to the OR to put him to sleep until we have converted the heart rhythm back to normal. The surgeon also wants to do an X-ray of his kidneys and urinary tract before taking him to the OR. We each have different clinical imperatives. I desperately want this guy out of my ER and in the OR ASAP. I think it is his only chance for survival and abhor what I judge to be unnecessary delays. But I am not the captain of this ship. In the trauma room the surgeon has that responsibility. Patients aren't always right, but when they keep begging to be kept alive and think their end is in sight you better listen.

I explain to him what is wrong, both problems, the GSW and the heart problem, and what we are going to do. He asks me to hold his hand. Comfort always, if possible. It is potentially the thing we are best at, so I take his hand. The incongruity of this strikes me harder this time. I order the sedation given and watch as his eyes glaze over and he slowly loses the grip on my hand. My face is the last thing he will ever see. We attempt the cardioversion three times. Each time, we are successful, but within a few seconds, the heart goes back to an unstable, rapid rhythm. His blood pressure just won't come up, no matter what we do. We are putting IV lines everywhere. We only have him for about fifteen minutes in the ER, then off he goes to the OR. I learn later that night he died during surgery, bleeding to death because the bullet had punctured his aorta.

I am filled with remorse. What should have been done differently? I only gave two units of blood in the ER. Should I have squeezed in more? Was it the failed cardioversion? Should I have pursued this problem at all? Should I have argued more strongly with the trauma surgeon that the X-ray wasted precious minutes? It could have been done in the OR after stopping the bleeding. Argued more strongly with anesthesia about delaying the case over the cardiac rhythm? I am tormented by so many questions and doubts.

I remain troubled about it for months. I think it was watching his eyes glaze over as he lost his grip on my hand that made it so difficult. If I close my eyes I can still see that moment. I am reminded that I need to relearn the lesson to limit too much connection with the patient or risk hurting myself. He wanted his mother, but my face was the last thing he saw.

For weeks after following busy crash shifts I feel exhausted, wanting only to go home to bed. Not invigorated as before. I am feeling like maybe I have seen enough mangled bodies and death. I am also starting to question if I have already seen too much. Cases harder and harder to forget. The lines between me and a patients tragedy blurring again. I know I have to let go of this perspective or I won't be able to continue. But can I? We shall see.

PC

MY NEW DRESS CODE

Dear Jack,

I am finally starting to feel at home in my new job at the trauma center. It really takes a while to be accepted, especially here where the staff is very cliquish. To the close-knit ER team, you remain "the new guy" for a long time. Even if you are the director, as I have been so named. I have now "arrived," though it has taken almost two years. I have to tell you about my new dress code. For me it's pretty exciting!

I hate the white coat. Even as a student doctor sporting this newly acquired badge of medicine, I hated it. The average student and ER doctor will wear the coat making rounds day after day. The coat gets increasingly dirtier and might get washed after a month or two. It might not. It just depends on whether anyone has vomited on you. I simply find it uncomfortable and too hot. I actually found working in my army BDUs and jungle boots far more comfortable and practical. They also got washed, starched, and pressed daily. Go figure.

When I left the army to work in one of the "nice civilian hospitals," I was expected to wear a shirt, tie, white coat, and best shoes. I gave it a try. I was unhappy--and uncomfortable. I persevered for a while. After a year, I am offered the medical directorship of the local trauma hospital, a public inner-city hospital considered by many to be the "real" ER in Central Texas.

They also expect me to dress like a doctor. Jeez. I was hoping for a more relaxed vibe.

After a few months at my new job, I lost the tie. Nobody says a word. Cool. Ties are just ridiculous, anyway. Soon thereafter, the white coat goes. I hate the damn thing. Still, not a peep. Weeks go by.

Even though the nurses all wear scrubs in the ER, the doctors don't. I decide to join the nurses and start working in scrubs. It's great. Loose, a little baggy, informal, and very comfortable. It is like going to work in your pajamas. And they are cleaned every day. I love the change. Nobody says a word. More weeks go by.

I have administrative days during which I do not see patients. I do paperwork and go from meeting to meeting. It's another sweltering summer in Central Texas so, bye-bye shoes. I'm putting on Birkenstocks. What's the worst thing that can happen? Get chastised, told to go home, and put on shoes? But…nobody says a word. I am feeling very happy at work. I love it.

Late August finally comes, and we are in the peak of the Texas heat. I decide things have gone so well, I will go for broke. I get ready for work, sporting a T-shirt, shorts, and sandals. My wife asks if I am really going to work in the hospital dressed like this. It gives me pause, and I rethink my position. I decide, yeah, I am. Maybe this time, I'll be told to go home and put a shirt and pants on, but at least for a while, I will be completely comfortable. Dressed just like a freshmen at Berkeley once again, I feel at home in these clothes. Off I go to work.

My trusty and beloved assistants, Rhonda and Heather, simply smile and laugh. They support me no matter what I do. I've been accepted into this mini-family. I have a great day of comfort, and nobody says a word. I may have found my dress code. The future looks bright.

Meet the new me. No more shirt and tie. I will make my laid-back look expected of me. "Oh, that's just Dr. Crocker and his way," they'll say. Nobody will tease, nobody will complain, whether I'm chief of emergency medicine, chief of staff, or a hospital board member. This is even better than going to work in pajamas.

They say, "The clothes make the man." I've got it made.

PC

HER LAST DOCTOR

Dear Jack,

I helped a woman die today. Well, it's not quite as stark as it sounds. It wasn't assisted suicide, a medical error or anything like that. I just helped to make her comfortable at the end of her life. I've always had this vision of people dying with dignity in the hospital or at home, family at the bedside, loving goodbyes, and then that final gasp. Lights out. The end of their story. It's not that way at all. It is usually kind of miserable.

There is often pain, confusion, and sometimes, horror. This poor woman was what we call an end-stage lung patient. Terminal. Nothing left to do for her except let her die peacefully or confine her to a ventilator for the remainder of her life. Most in her situation die fighting for breath, like a person who dove underwater, stayed too long, and swims frantically to the surface to breathe. You know the feeling, that overwhelming hunger for air. They sometimes struggle just as miserably for weeks on end.

For this patient, though, we helped spare her that agony. The nurses seemed a bit angry for some reason, like we had not done everything we could. Well, we did. It just didn't include her final weeks on a ventilator. I can't understand their feelings. Don't they also strive to follow primum non nocere? Chronically suffering patients can be the worst, and their suffering can break your heart.

My first introduction to pulmonary patients was at the VA hospital when I started my career. I was warned what it would be like, but you never know till you get there. Basically, the VA respiratory ward is a home for those with severe, chronic respiratory disease that waxes and wanes while the patients wait for that final fatal infection. We call these patients "lungers." They come in two basic varieties, blue bloaters and pink puffers. Their diseases are man-made and self-inflicted. Years of smoking inexorably do their damage. The end result is one of the two conditions, depending on whether the person's skin coloring has turned pink or blue. For the pink puffers, it's emphysema, in which the lung tissues are gradually destroyed, impairing the delivery of oxygen to the blood but not obstructing airflow. These pink puffers are usually thin and often emaciated, causing their skin to turn a sallow pink until near the end. For the blue bloaters, the disease is mainly the result of chronic inflammation and over-production of mucus secretions, with some asthma-like airway constriction, as well. While their lung tissue is also destroyed, the main manifestation is the inability to move air in and out of the lungs, kind of like having a chronic asthma attack. They are often overweight, barrel-chested individuals who, toward the end of their disease, take on a blue skin hue. The medical name for this coloration is cyanosis. It represents the inability to deliver sufficient oxygen to the blood to meet the body's needs.

Both types of patients have a miserable final exit. At first, their disease is marked by only a chronic cough or shortness of breath while being active. Medicines help. There is usually a long series of acute bronchitis episodes during which they are worse but can get better with antibiotics and other medications. Finally, they are on an array of medicines, which often include daily antibiotics and steroids. You see, they know and we know that eventually one of these episodes of bronchitis or pneumonia will doom them.

We do all we can to prevent these episodes. And the typical patient will keep smoking regardless of our admonishments. Cigarettes are incredibly addictive as our patients keep smoking, despite how awful they feel. Frequently, they experience years of slow worsening and multiple hospitalizations during which they fight for air. Ultimately, they can only live on a ventilator, and most refuse this option. In the end, they all die fighting for breath.

The VA respiratory ward is where they come during their acute episodes. We mainly treat ex-soldiers who have government benefits for health care. I often wonder, why did these patients do this to themselves? Did two packs a day really seem that good all those years? For this? Room after room of them, two to a room, they sit on the edge of their beds. It's always the same posture, leaning forward on their bedside stand, fighting for air. The bloaters are the worst somehow. They all have little basins of phlegm at their side to catch their daily cough production. During acute episodes, it can be tremendous. Literally cups and cups of yellow-green slimy spit. We call this stuff "oysters." It is so disgusting we have to joke about it to face it. The phlegm does bear a superficial resemblance to a cup of raw oysters. At any rate, they all have their basins. The all get breathing treatments every few hours. After breathing treatments, they feel better for a little while, and then we repeat the cycle. They do this until they get well enough to return home, or they die. In the end, of course, we could keep them alive longer by placing them on ventilators. Almost all have gone through home oxygen and multiple daily breathing treatments. A ventilator is all that's left. It's only a temporary reprieve from death for the few who want it. Occasionally, the ER is viewed as a culprit for placing such patients on a ventilator. We get a patient in severe distress, frequently unconscious and blue. We don't know the patient, and they don't come with a sign that says, "Do not put me on a ventilator." So, on they go, making the situation worse for them. Primum non nocere. It's so easy for that simple guidance to go awry.

My patient is sixty-eight years old, but she looks ninety. I received a call from her lung specialist before she even arrived. He told me her story, her refusals for further intervention, and a planned consultation with hospice. A whole plan for making her comfortable during her final days. The original plan is now in limbo because here she is in the ER, struggling for breath. Her doctor's final words to me were, "Please, no ventilator." He said he would be by to see her in an hour or so.

After that call, I tell the charge nurse that when the patient arrives, make sure the chart comes to me. I don't want a mistake made and find she has been placed on a ventilator. Our ER is a big one with sometimes as many as six attendings and multiple residents, so I feel it's essential I get the chart. I learn my patient has actually just arrived and is down in crash. So, I hustle down to meet her.

She's in the usual position, hunched over a tray table at the side of the bed, struggling to breathe. This position actually does provide them with some slight relief as it helps more fully expand the lung tissue that's left. A breathing treatment has just been started and I put my arm across her shoulders to greet her. She offers a weak but welcome smile as a thank you. I hope she understands I will take care of her as she wishes. No ventilator, just comfort care.

I also let her know what her doctor has told me about her. Her struggles, her bravery, and her final acceptance. She simply listens, trying to breathe. I confirm with her that she still doesn't want a ventilator. That she has really decided on comfort care. And she manages to gasp, "yes." It is a sad moment for me. But I, too, accept that her time has come, knowing that a ventilator could prolong her life a short while and only offer a very slim chance she might, someday, get off of it. She doesn't want that or the suffering that would go with it.

My mind drifts to how much more humanely we treat our pets. We love them, and they become part of our families. And when they reach a stage of life in which they are suffering, we take care of it for them. Yes, it's a sad trip to the vet, with tearful goodbyes and a kiss on the head. And then the vet quickly and peacefully ends their suffering. Today, that's my goal: making my patient's passing less traumatic.

I do provide some high-dose breathing treatments and multiple medications for her, hoping she could become well enough to return home or to a hospice bed. I also give her a small dose of morphine.

The morphine helps tremendously. I see how it lessens her anxiety and the sensation of being starved for air. She thanks me. She wants more. And I answer, "In a little bit." As I said, this will not be assisted suicide, rather comfort care. At this moment, though, those definitions seem greatly blurred.

As promised, her lung doctor comes to see her. He is a top-notch doctor I have worked with for years and he has been down this road many times. He spends some time with her and holds her hand. It is actually very touching to see him like this, in a role I have never witnessed him performing. I think he is doing a great job with her and move closer to the bedside.

He confirms everything they have discussed previously. He reiterates that the end is very near and that her only desire is to be made comfortable. And we all agree that this will be the approach for the next couple of hours. If she improves, she will go to a bed upstairs and to hospice care tomorrow. If she doesn't, she will die here in the ER, with me watching over her. I have learned that she is all alone in the world. She has no kin and no close friends. I will be her last friend.

Her doctor leaves us to go see other patients. I sit with her for a few minutes and ask if she would like a little more morphine. And, of course, she says yes. So, I order another small dose. It brings her further relief, and I tell her I will be back when the next breathing treatment finishes to check on her. I have moved her to a more private corner bed but ask if she would like the curtains left open so she can see out. She says yes, just for a bit. I go see my other patients.

When I return, it is obvious that not only are the treatments not working, she looks a bit worse. She also seems a bit sleepy. I believe carbon dioxide is building up in her blood, high levels of which will have this sedating effect. Ultimately, the carbon dioxide level will get so elevated, it will be fatal. I know now I will be her last doctor, as she will never make it to that hospice bed. She asks for a little more morphine, and I say yes.

I stay at the bedside patting her hand, trying to give some final comfort. I give her the last small dose of morphine, and she says she feels better, even comfortable. She now asks me to please pull the curtain closed. I do, and then I sit back down next to her. I can't let her die alone behind a curtain.

She is lying back on the bed, with her head elevated. Her eyes are closed, but she is still awake. She says she is ready to rest. We both know this is her euphemism for dying. She asks me to stay till she falls asleep. I tell her I'm not leaving, and in minutes, she is asleep.

I am thankful that the ER has been slow today and that I have been able to spend more than with her than I would with almost any other patient. After all, I am all she has. I can't help but feel sad. Her breathing stops in another five minutes. The heart monitor continues to beep with each heart-beat for about fifteen minutes, and then flatlines. She is gone.

I call her doctor to let him know she has just died and won't need any hospice bed. He thanks me and says goodbye.

As I finish up her paperwork and death certificate, I think again about the definitions of comfort care and assisted suicide. I consider that, in prac-tice, they are actually different, but in the end, they achieve similar aims.

I know my patient was grateful for my help and for those small doses of morphine. I hope when my time comes, I get the same treatment. I know I have done the right thing, but I am saddened nonetheless. I understood her wishes and followed them.

What I cannot understand is the reaction I get from staff members. It seems they wanted me to put her on a ventilator and send her to ICU. Yes, that would have been the easier route, but that would have failed my patient and dishonored her wishes. More care is not necessarily better care.

I walk over and pick up the next chart. It's been a sad ordeal, but I am glad I was there for her and working today.

PC

RITES OF SPRING

Dear Jack,

    It's finally springtime in Central Texas. The mornings are cool and crisp. Out in the nearby Hill Country, a carpet of green has pushed up from the valleys to the hilltops. Bluebonnets, Indian paintbrush, and Firewheels are everywhere. Lots of other smaller forbs with little tiny flowers compete for attention. The live oaks have dropped their leaves, and new growth is everywhere. Red oaks seemingly overnight are draped in bright green cover. And the stately bald cypress trees that provide a canopy to protect us from the Texas sun in July, August, and September while we swim in the river are also now covered in green. This explosion of life and rebirth following winter is simply beautiful. But all of this beauty comes at a steep price. A sad, morbid rite of spring passage has also arrived. Today is our community's first pediatric drowning of the year.

    It's afternoon, and the ER is hopping. The winter kept us jam-packed with flu, bronchiolitis, and simple colds. Thankfully, that's over, but it is still busy. The encoder that we use to alert us to incoming ambulance units emits a tone that tells of yet another incoming EMS unit. The details that follow make us shudder. Emergency Medical Services is in route with a five-year-old; CPR is in progress. A drowning. ETA is only two minutes as the pool is near the hospital. We assemble in the resuscitation room and don our gowns and gloves. The quick arrival time gives us a reason to hope. CPR in progress, though, is usually a grim predictor of the outcome. After just ten minutes of CPR the outlook for a good outcome drops precipitously. But two minutes of CPR? We are not optimistic but we can hope.

Suddenly, the ambulance crew bursts in. Paramedics are compressing a small, delicate chest, with bag ventilation in progress. It's odd the things that cross my mind. I notice he is still in his brightly colored swimsuit. Sandy blond hair covers his perfect head. A really cute kid. He reminds me of a Norman Rockwell painting on an old Saturday Evening Post. Close up of his smiling face, shirtless in bib overalls, a barn behind him, and chewing a stem of green grass playfully poking out of a broad smile. But now his eyes stare vacantly. Pupils are dilated, with only a hint of reaction to light.

We go to work. A quick endotracheal tube is placed so we can get him better ventilated. I see some slightly bloody froth coming from his trachea during the procedure. It's not a good sign. It means he has aspirated the pool water into his lungs. I'm already a bit morose. The nurses scramble for an IV site and a partner works to place an intraosseous line, one that's directly inserted in the bone marrow used when veins collapse and we can't start a regular IV. It will deliver medication and fluids. These tasks are accomplished quickly here. Our nurses are very good. They are pediatric specialty nurses, and we are in a pediatric trauma center. If our patient has any chance at all, it is here.

Some medications can safely go down the endotracheal tube and get quickly absorbed into the central circulation. It's our best option when we don't have time or a peripheral IV line. This little boy is flat-lining, so there isn't a second to spare. I order a double dose of epinephrine down the tube. It is the strongest cardiac stimulant there is, and if anything will restart his quiet heart, it is this. The respiratory tech bag ventilates a bit more rapidly to force the medication down into his lungs. CPR continues.

Three minutes later, he is still flatlining. We have peripheral lines now, and I order another dose of epinephrine. Within another minute or so, his heart begins to beat. The team allows itself a little enthusiasm as we get a weak pulse. We start dopamine, and his blood pressure improves. His once cold, white skin begins to take on some color.

It's the best we can do, but I fear it is not enough. Most likely, we started too late in the game for a good result. I wonder if I have done the right thing. What will his future be? How long was his brain starved of oxygen? Our guiding dictum is *primum non nocere*. First, do no harm. Is attempting resuscitation on a patient with fixed and dilated pupils harm? Maybe. But I can't watch a child die without trying. Decisions that were black and white when I was younger now seem gray. Is this wisdom from years of practice? Or simple indecision. I don't know.

I now have a little time to talk to the paramedics and a witness. This will give me a much better idea of how this will end. What I hear leaves me shaken. He was in a crowded pool with a bunch of other kids having fun. Maybe even the first swim of the year. Lifeguards are present, watching for misbehavior or the kid that starts struggling in the water. Every parent receives a false sense of safety and security when a lifeguard's on hand. It's a widely believed myth that the lifeguard has time to save a drowning person. It's another myth that the typical drowning includes a scream for help, splashing wildly, a kid obviously in distress. The grim truth is, most drownings are silent. The child simply slips below the surface, inhales the water he was enjoying seconds ago, and never raises his head again. A silent death among bystanders. It is a sickening reconstruction of his death. But it is exactly what happened. This beautiful boy was found limp on the bottom of the pool.

The parents come into the room. They have been standing outside watching but now are by their child's side. I explain what we are doing to help him. I'm not sure how much they actually hear, even though the room is quiet. At times like this, you simply can't process any other information than the sight of your child on a gurney, in a trauma room, after CPR. It is a terrible sight. They are sobbing. As they look at me in shock and disbelief, I tell them the only thing I can. There is hope. But no optimism. A slim chance is all I can extend.

The intensivist (a critical-care specialist) and I discuss possible hypothermia, a process of cooling the body to preserve brain function. I am in favor. Hypothermia sometimes works wonders, protecting the brain from its own inflammatory response and biochemical transmitters that become activated to complete brain death. The intensivist objects. Research supporting hypothermia mostly is based on adults after cardiac arrests stemming from heart disease, not drowning. I argue the brain can't tell the difference. I realize hypothermia is not harmless and has its own complications. But I want to go for broke, as it seems there is not much more to lose. The outcome is he will decide when they get to the pediatric ICU. *Primum non nocere.* First, do no harm. And with that, this little boy is wheeled out of the ER -- and out of our lives. But not from our memory.

Everyone is thinking of his or her own children. Are they safe? Are they swimming at a neighbor's house or a public pool? Kids who may have misbehaved today and were promised a spanking later will get a reprieve. Or they will simply get a hug they don't understand. If it's a boy over six, it will be an embarrassingly long hug. He won't understand until he has a child of his own.

As I write in the child's chart, I think about my own mortality. Average lifespan of the U.S. male is 78.6 years. I count maybe nineteen more springtimes for me. A distressingly small number. I try 85 years, as I am healthy, active, and lack bad habits. Twenty-five more springs. Still a distressingly small number. I love the sunrise, so I decide to count sunrises. Twenty-five years times 365 days per year and I get 9,125 more sunrises. This sounds a bit better. I think of yet a better number. The number of times I can be with my wife and daughter and tell them I love them. Limitless. Perhaps this is the number I should shoot for. The truth, of course, is none of us has any idea how much time we will have, regardless of how we break it down.

Sadly, my patient's story ends as I had feared. A cerebral perfusion study the next day shows zero blood flow to this precious young brain.

Simply put, his brain is dead. I don't know what happened after that. Perhaps he was an organ donor and gave the gift of life to others. I hope so.

I have been one of the hospital spokespersons for water safety and drowning prevention. Every spring at this time, the local news media covers our story. Water safety requires parents' eyes on children without interruption. No reading. No summer daydreaming. No phone. The parent must be only seconds away from aiding his or her own child, lifeguard or not.

Life in the ER can sometimes be grim. Some shifts come filled with broken bodies, death, and destruction. Other days are better. We see humanity at it's worst and at it's best. Most of us love what we do — the chance to save a life. We simply can't leave such a challenging place, no matter how sad it gets.

Hardly a week passes, and like clockwork, we get our second drowning.

PC

A TRIP BACK FROM THE DEAD

Dear Jack,

I was working up a patient with a bleeding ulcer in the crash area when the EMS encoder gave us this alert: STAR Flight en route with a bad MVA, shorthand for motor vehicle accident. For EMS to send its helicopter unit to a crash scene generally means we will see serious, if not life-threatening, injuries. I note that, for some reason, the encoder sounds particularly shrill to me today, an unwelcome disturbance to an otherwise routine morning.

One of the flight victims is a seventeen-year-old who is hypotensive, sweating, and confused. More victims are on the way, including this teenager's father. I stop and wonder for a second if some family will lose a father and a son today. Life is fragile. And sometimes cruel. This reality wears on all of us at times. For ER staff, it can lead to depression, substance abuse, and early professional burnout. If you dwell on the tragedies you see all too often, they will ultimately consume you. It ruins careers. Burnout is a real concern from which I strive to protect myself. As I've mentioned before, learning to care for patients while not being too involved in caring about them is a difficult balancing act to master. But in this environment, it's essential.

The STAR Flight crew reports that it has already given two liters of saline to the teenage patient, with no response in blood pressure. It's still eighty over fifty and getting dangerously low when they ask if they can give the two units of packed red blood cells they have onboard. I say yes. I trust this crew. Many have been previous ER nurses here and I know them and the other crewmembers well. They are the best paramedics and flight nurses I have ever worked with. So yes, squeeze in the blood as fast as you can, I tell them. They are still about fifteen minutes out.

This presentation already sounds like a Class IV hemorrhage to me, the worst grade there is. It amounts to rapidly losing forty percent or more of your blood volume. So, in an average adult, that loss amounts to over two quarts. That's a lot of blood.

Even with rapid blood replacement, this kind of hemorrhage can kill. Your body goes into an irreversible shock state and starts shutting down, despite our best therapy. He is young, and if I were to bet on this one, I always give the young the best odds. They survive traumas that would certainly kill an older person.

Our trauma rooms are always fully set up and ready to receive patients. The trauma team has been paged. All of our equipment is ready. The trauma surgeon is already in the OR doing a case and says to call him back when the patient arrives. All we can do now is wait.

Just as we hear the helicopter landing, the encoder makes a sound we dread hearing. Our patient has just suffered a cardiac arrest. Damn, I think, only fifty yards from possible salvation, and now he is dying, if not already dead. A cardiac arrest resulting from trauma almost always spells a patient's demise. The morning has suddenly become more than a bit depressing.

When they roll into the ER, one of the crew is riding the gurney doing chest compressions, another is ventilating him with an Ambu bag. He has already been intubated and is ready to be placed on a ventilator. Good. One less thing for me to worry about doing. First the ABCs, as always. Confirm tube placement. Confirm breath sounds in each side of his chest. A collapsed lung could make it impossible to resuscitate him if not treated rapidly. Pressure can build up in the chest, preventing blood flow through the heart and causing death.

I quickly placed what's called an introducer into his subclavian vein. It's a large blood vessel under the collarbone and easily accessed, most of the time. This introducer is, more or less, a very large IV line, almost as big around as a soda straw. The staff hangs more blood from our rapid infuser, which can give blood at a rate of almost a liter every minute or two. It even warms it up to body temperature that fast. The nurses start two other IV lines. Normal saline is being pressure pumped into both lines. As soon as we can, I order an ampule of IV epinephrine. Maybe we can restart his heart with that. It's given by IV push, and I'll be damned: We immediately get a pulse and blood pressure. Only a brief five minutes or less of CPR gives me hope for this kid. If the surgeon can get the internal bleeding controlled quickly, maybe a lot of hope.

I have the trauma surgeon paged again to come STAT. Order emergency plasma infusions, more blood, get a blood gas, and a bunch of labs. Trauma care in wars has taught us that we must replace the blood plasma as well as the blood cells. The plasma contains the proteins that actually cause your blood to clot in a wound. I wonder again just why we ever abandoned giving whole blood, which contains blood cells and plasma, to patients with major blood loss. Early in my career, that's what we did, and it seemed obvious to us it worked the best.

I also wonder about the realities of practicing medicine when that which is "true" one year, becomes "false" a few years later, and then flips back down the road. This has always puzzled me. Is clinical research really that hard to coax the right answer from the first time? I also think of all the times we have been told of a new wonder drug that turns out to actually be a bad one and patients are unwittingly hurt. A primum non nocere fail. Meperidine, once touted as a non-addictive solution to morphine, turned out to be horribly addicting. Worse yet, it was found to have toxic metabolites. Terfenadine, an antihistamine, worked great for allergies but also caused patient deaths from cardiac problems. Aminophylline, once considered an absolute necessity to use when treating severe asthma patients, was later found to do very little to actually help asthma. And it was poison for the heart. The list goes on and on. And all after assurances from the manufacturers, "independent" researchers and the FDA that they were all safe and effective.

I order a quick chest and pelvis X-ray. So much to do and so little time to prevent irreversible shock. The blood gas returns, and to my relief, it is only moderately acidotic. This means he had been maintaining a better circulation than I imagined. If the blood acid gets too high, this can also sometimes not be recovered from. His hematocrit though is only six percent! It should be more like forty-five percent. Roughly, he had maybe fifteen percent of his blood still in his body when he arrived. This poor kid was running on empty.

We continue our work, and in a few minutes, the surgeon is here. He tells us the trauma room in the OR is ready and off the patient goes. I briefly explain the course of events to him. He is an unflappable, died-in-the-wool Texan. A senior surgeon who I respect and even operated with once. Never loses his cool and is loved by all the staff. He simply says, "good work" and leaves the room. I move over to the treatment side as the other patients have been triaged there and that doc can probably use the help.

Only a few minutes have passed, and I am in the charting room review-ing my next patient's chart. I hear a phone ring and look over to see my sur-geon standing at the bedside of a patient who has been placed nearby. The surgeon is taking a call, probably the OR saying they are ready to start the case. Then I hear him say, "The kid had a cardiac arrest but Crocker and his crew pulled his ass out of the fire. Now I need to operate." I hear nothing else. I am frantically waving my hands trying to get his attention. Shut up, I am thinking. The patient on the gurney next to him is the kid's injured father and doesn't yet know what has happened to his son. My surgeon has no clue, unfortunately, and it's too late. He is off to the OR. Damn, I wish I could have prevented the father from hearing that brief conversation.

I can't imagine what this man is thinking. The shock of hearing such news about your child must be overwhelming. Not just sad but crushing. I consider how I would feel in that position, flat on a gurney with my own injuries, hearing my child had a cardiac arrest and is now in the OR. Horrible.

I stop what I am doing and go over to the father's bedside. His injuries are not life-threatening. I explain in detail what has happened, what we did in the brief fifteen minutes or so I was taking care of his son, and just why I have hope. And why he should, too. I hope he feels a little better, even though he could be facing a possible tragedy.

A few hours later, I learn that his son's liver and spleen were bleeding profusely. The surgeon removed the spleen and packed the liver with gauze to stop the immediate bleeding. It will be dealt with more thoroughly tomorrow. This is called damage-control surgery. You don't finish the entire job, just stop the life threats. Then, you wait a day, giving the body a chance to recover a bit and adjust from the shock state. We save more lives this way. Again, emergency medicine practitioners learned this from documented experience on the battlefield. Just one more incongruity, I think, that so many lost in war are now saving civilian lives.

The teenager's CT brain looked good too. No obvious trauma. Blood pressure is now stable. He is going to make it. Because he was young, and lucky, and got the best care available in our region, he beat the odds.

I never learn just how long he was in the hospital or even hear from him or his father again. I would have liked for them to know the details, sit down with them, and talk about how lucky they were. But I never will. This is not the province of ER medicine. We treat, and then they are gone.

I hope this lucky young man has done something wonderful with his second chance. Something tells me he has. And I am satisfied, even happy, with that bit of fantasy.

PC

THERE'S SOMETHING HAPPENING HERE

Dear Jack,

Something has been bothering me lately. It's that dictum, primum non nocere. First, do no harm. On the surface it seems so straightforward, but in actual practice it can prove a tall order to follow. As the years of practice fly by, that simple guide seems even more elusive. What is, and what isn't harm can be hidden in various shades of gray. It's an ill-defined, sometimes circumstantial blurry mess that I can't always bring into focus. Let me explain.

A few weeks ago, I was working in the children's ER and received a call from one of the clinics. A four-year-old girl who had stitches placed in her scalp was ready to have them removed. The trouble was, they couldn't get them out. It wasn't too busy, so I said, send her over and I will take a look. Usually with a little calm explanation and some special little blunt tipped scissors, the stitches can easily be removed--and painlessly at that. I am suspicious I'm not hearing the full story.

A bit later, my patient arrives. I can tell from a glance she has been crying and is frightened to be here. I wave to her and smile, and she gives a tentative wave back. It's my way of letting her know I am her friend. That I won't hurt her or repeat whatever has happened earlier in the clinic. That no harm will come to her here. Once my nurse has her situated in bed I go over to see her.

A quick look at her scalp now clarifies why she is here. Her partially healed wound is oozing blood from several spots. Spots where the clinic doctor had tried to dig out her stitches. Stitches that were originally placed too tightly, and now are deeply embedded in her scalp. Damn. I can imagine what she has been through already this morning. And it has not paved the way for their simple quick removal.

I explain to her and her mother what the problem is and my proposed solution. I will offer a brief sedation so that I can remove the stitches without her struggling or having pain. I do this all talking directly to my little patient, glancing at mom every few seconds to make sure she understands. I gain more ground with a child this age talking to them directly and not ignoring them, as if they are an observer. They are the patient, after all, and understand a lot at this age. As I leave to go enter the orders I actually get a "bye" and a little smile from her. Progress.

My nurse does a great job of starting her IV and getting things set up. Not even an audible whimper from the little girl. I walk over and we prepare to begin as I give her another explanation that the bad part is over, nothing will hurt, and that she will wake up ready to go home. My nurse and I do our pre-procedure check. That's a safety step to insure we have the right patient, know exactly what we are going to do, and have rechecked the dose of sedative. I give the order to push the medication in, prepared for the usual four- or five-minute wait till she goes to sleep. But something is clearly wrong.

Within seconds of the medication being given to this sweet little girl, she is deeply unconscious. The hair on my neck erect as I realize something is wrong, perhaps terribly wrong. While keeping a close eye on her breathing, oxygen saturation, and heart rate, I ask my nurse how much medication was given. I try to remain calm, even casual, as mom is already looking worried. I am told, "Twenty-six milligrams, exactly as ordered".

I consider maybe this child is simply more sensitive than usual to the medication. Maybe. I know this nurse well and trust her, but I ask again. "How much medication was given? Please recheck." I get the same answer,

"Twenty-six milligrams, exactly." Ok I think, I will watch her very closely. I am worried there could be an unforeseen complication occurring right before my eyes.

It only takes me about five minutes to do the job. The stitches were deeply embedded and partially covered with new skin. I cause a little more bleeding. I tell Mom all is fine, it will heal well, and gently apply some pressure with a gauze pad to the bleeding areas. While I am doing this, I start to think about that dictum, my guide: First, do no harm.

I wonder if a sedation had been done when she first presented with this fairly large laceration if today's events could have been avoided. Would the sutures have been tied too tight had she been sedated rather than being placed during what I am sure was a struggle? I picture an ER tech and her mom trying to hold her down while the doctor fought to close the wound. Did the decision to close it without sedation end in harm? And that led to a second painful experience in the clinic during the attempted suture removal. Now she is in this inexplicably deep sedation that might turn dire. Is even more harm in progress?

Ten minutes or so pass. My nurse is cleaning up the suture tray and preparing discharge instructions. I stay with the patient watching her breathing making sure she is stable. Usually, after such a sedation, she would already be waking up a bit by now and responding to stimulation. As I listen to her heart and lungs I surreptitiously give her arm a pinch. Not even a flinch. Omigod, something is definitely wrong.

I wave my nurse over to the bed. I whisper to her to go back and go through exactly how she drew up the medications and check that dose again. I explain my concern to Mom. I am not going to try to hide what is going on and assure her that her daughter will be fine. But I am worried and mortified that something horrible has gone wrong. Despite our safety check, something is quite wrong.

After what seemed like forever my nurse returns red-faced and a bit shaken. She motions me over, knowing that I will not take more than a couple of steps from my unresponsive patient. She confesses that an error was made in drawing up the medication and thinks the child has received three to five times the requested dose.

Ketamine, the medication at issue, is thankfully, very forgiving. Patients retain spontaneous breathing and airway protection on their own--at the usual doses that is. At this dose, maybe not. Her breathing has remained just fine, but I am worried about a possible aspiration while she is this deeply sedated. This is when saliva or stomach contents seep into the lungs because the patient can't protect their own airway. Should I intubate her, put down a breathing tube to protect her lungs? My morning has gone from a nice slow one to a mess. Primum non nocere? Have we made a bad situation much worse?

I elect to stay at her bedside however long it takes for her to awaken. After a little while she is arousable with a little stimulation. She will be able to go home in a couple of hours after all, unscathed, despite the error.

Medication is a key way harm can be done to a patient. On the surface, decisions to prescribe should be easy. But all medications have side effects, some of them serious. Simple ibuprofen can cause a bleeding stomach. An antibiotic can cause an allergic reaction. Are these risks always worth the presumed benefit? Are the common prescribing practices really consistent with our guiding principle? Do we do harm with medications more than we realize? Today, it all could have ended up quite badly.

Using a certain number has become a popular way to help us measure the effectiveness of the medications and treatments we prescribe. It is called the NNT, the number (of patients) needed to treat before we can derive a measurable benefit for one patient. It's part of "evidence-based medicine," and the numbers available now are shocking.

First, consider a prescription for antibiotics for strep throat, surely a simple and obvious problem needing antibiotics, right? Well, the evidence-based approach actually reveals that we must treat four patients with antibiotics for even one to show an actual clinical benefit. That's an NNT of four. Further, the evidence shows that the benefit of giving antibiotics for the patient's pain relief and "back to work" status is a mere sixteen hours sooner versus doing nothing. Were the side effects and possible complications caused by our prescription worth this benefit? Only twenty-five percent of patients are better off than they would have been if we had done nothing. And the NNT for antibiotics and strep throat is one of the most straightforward for which we have data. The treatment of conjunctivitis with antibiotics, a common eye infection, has a NNT of twelve. There's a lot more.

The new drugs to fight influenza are another great example. The flu is a common illness and medication is often taken as a prescribing option. When these medications are used to prevent influenza, the patient's chances of reporting flu symptoms are actually exactly the same as if they had been given a placebo! There is a modest decrease in the number of patients whose tests show they have acquired the flu virus, from nearly nine percent to four percent. This gives an NNT of twenty. So, one patient in twenty is actually helped. But every one of those twenty were put at risk of side effects. The use of bone strengthening bisphosphonates for osteoporosis has an NNT of 100, even when the patient has a history of prior broken bones. So, they help one in a hundred people. What are we doing with such unhelpful medications?

Statin drugs that have become synonymous with "preventing heart attacks and strokes" have an NNT of sixty for heart attacks and 268 for strokes! If you have known coronary disease, the NNT is thirty-nine. The NNT for daily aspirin to prevent a first heart attack, if you are healthy, is 1,667. And these are medications with serious and frequent side effects. Intra-cardiac stents for stable angina have an astounding NNT of 50. And every one of those patients are placed on medications known to cause bleeding problems for a year after stent placement. I am sure you see the basis for my ruminations on primum non nocere.

The few medications and procedures we actually have the NNT data to look at is small. However, it is assumed that medications with an NNT of four or less are reasonably good. If the NNT is between four and fifteen, the medication is considered to be potentially good. A higher NNT than fifteen puts it at questionable value. Think of it this way. If you were considering hiring a carpenter that had to swing his hammer fifteen times to drive a single nail would you want him working for you?

It makes me realize we know far less about what we think we are accomplishing than what we actually accomplish. And all the time, we are putting the patient at risk. Is this at all consistent with primum non nocere?

The information we are gaining from evidenced-based medicine is nothing short of astounding. Unfortunately, a lot of it is ignored by many physicians. What will we learn in the future about what we do? Will it be even more harm is revealed? I won't be surprised.

So far, the data is limited to prescribing and some procedures. None of it yet addresses the day to day decisions we make, believing we are acting in the patient's interest. Those are often more important.

So medical decision-making become more and more of a quandary, covered in those shades of gray I mentioned earlier. When I consider the kind of care I intend to provide, my decisions becomes more and more fuzzy to me. If questioned, I generally will tell patients that my proposed therapy is the same as what I would do for my family. I can only do my best, given present evidence, even though I know that a standard therapy could be proven next week to be totally ineffective—and even risky for the patient.

I thought medical decision-making would get easier, with years of experience. Not harder. I thought our admonition to first, do no harm would become a clearer target, easier and easier to achieve.

I was just wrong about that.

PC

KIDS SWALLOW THE DARNDEST THINGS

Dear Jack,

Do you remember the Art Linkletter show, Kids Say the Darndest Things? I'm here to tell you they also swallow the darndest things. And their ears and nose are not spared their experiments, either. Anything that will fit in the selected orifice has been tried at one time or another.

These objects usually cause quite a fuss at home. The parents rush to the ER with little Johnny, who, by comparison, is usually in no distress. The parents clamor for a doctor, imagining the emergency surgery that's now required. It usually doesn't matter what the object was. The parents figure, if it wasn't food, it doesn't belong there and must be removed medically.

In actual practice, if whatever the kid swallowed made it past the airway and into the stomach, our approach is almost always the same: Wait and see. There are, of course, exceptions. If the swallowed item has lodged in the esophagus, then it will need to come out but this can usually be done with a scope that doesn't require an incision. Button batteries and magnets also are usually handled differently. But marbles, coins, little rubber balls, bottle caps, beads, bobby pins, straight pins, safety pins almost always come out the other end.

I had one overwrought mother that I could not seem to calm. Her son had swallowed a little plastic soldier. Not even an inch long. But she would not be calmed. Finally, I asked, "Just what is your specific concern?" She drew close, looks me in the eye, and utterly serious, says, "Well this army man was carrying a gun!" I hardly knew what to say. Pointing out it was an unloaded plastic gun clearly wasn't going to help. She left angry and dissatisfied with my assurances, saying she'd go see a "real doctor" somewhere else.

And then there are the siblings who feed objects to each other. Usually the older brother tempting the younger with some object. You know, "Give it to Mikey. He will eat anything." And that was my first case on this particular evening shift.

Mom and three kids are awaiting my arrival in the exam room. The chart says she thinks one of the older kids coaxed the four-year-old to swallow a piece of rubber. When I introduce myself, she is frantic. I get a history from her and question the kids. All of the children deny Mom's supposition. My patient is in no distress and has a normal exam. I ask Mom why she is so convinced that her little girl has swallowed a piece of rubber. Her answer, "Because I can see it sticking out of her butt!"

This is a new one on me. I am a bit chagrined after my explanations and assurances fail to calm her. I now imagine a quick end to this case as I suddenly remember I do have experience with this scenario after all. My dog ate part of a towel once, and two days later, about four inches of it was protruding from his read end. I gently pulled. And pulled. And almost two full feet of towel came out of my dog. So, I know how to handle this one.

I explain to my little patient what we are going to do. Mommy will be by your side. And I just need to take a look at her bottom. Without a skipped beat, she lifts her dress, removes her underwear, and rolls over. Well, at least she is going to make it easy for me.

And there it is. About two inches of rubber protruding from her anus. It looks like a small narrow rubber cylinder. At this point, my right hand, almost without direct command, moves confidently toward the offending bit of rubber. Apparently, it has is planned to simply pull it out. I stop it just in time. This whole case is striking me as odd, I mean, odder than it already sounds. I turn on an overhead surgical light for a closer look. Yup, a piece of rubber. Sorry I doubted you Mom.

And then I notice irregularities in its surface. What? I position a second light to move in as close as I can without having Child Protective Services called. I now can see it has a smoothly shaped blunt end and a couple of very small perforations. Very neatly beveled perforations. This isn't a plain piece of rubber at all. But what is it?

At times like this, I have learned to exercise restraint and rethink things. Don't act hastily and regret it. I review everything again with mom who seems relieved I now believe her. One of those guilty siblings has indeed fed her daughter a piece of rubber and there will be hell to pay by one of them. I order an X-ray of her abdomen. If nothing else, it will give me a little more time to think. This foreign object strikes me as simply too weird to try and remove without more information. Something else may be up, but I have no idea what. Primum non nocere. Proceed with caution when facing the unknown.

Twenty minutes later, the patient and X-ray film return. I take it over to the viewing box and am stunned. The little piece of rubber is a couple of feet long and vanishes off the top of the X-ray into her chest. And then it dawns on me. This little piece of rubber is actually a ventriculoperitoneal shunt! It's a tube inserted into the brain and then tunneled down under the skin to drain excess spinal fluid into her abdomen. I go the bedside and ask mom if she has one. She says yes.

What the hell has happened? These shunts are not supposed to come out of the anus. They aren't even supposed to be connected to the intestines at all. But, somehow, likely very slowly, this tube must have eroded through her colon wall and entered into her digestive tract. Miraculously, her colon contents didn't leak into her abdomen. The movement of stool through her colon has finally brought it out her anus with a bowel movement.

I am so damn glad I stopped my errant hand from simply attempting to pull this little tube out. That would have been a mess. When things aren't adding up in a case you just have to force yourself to take a step back. That pause allows you to break the grip of diagnostic momentum and premature diagnostic closure, the fast thinking that leads to cognitive bias. Two of the most common errors in medicine. And I almost fell into the trap.

Happily, the girl's surgery the next day was uneventful. The tube was removed, a new one was placed, and she will go home in a couple of days. And nobody got a spanking for feeding her that piece of rubber.

PC

I MEET A GHOUL

Dear Jack,

I was working in the Children's ER last week and had a remarkable case I want to tell you about. Let me set the scene:

It's morning, and we get a phone call from hospital security. A man in the parking lot called that office to say he had sudden chest pain. He was parked somewhere near the entrance, he had told them. And then the phone line went dead. The staff, pushing a gurney, run out of the ER and down the hall toward the entrance to try and find him. We get a lot of calls to respond to someone who has fallen or fainted in the hospital, and it usually turns out to be a big nothing. So, I continue working without another thought about the drama that's heading my way. Hearing that the line went dead was a little worrisome, but cellphones often drop calls.

Several minutes later, security calls back. The man has been found, staff is on their way back, CPR in progress. I immediately think, fat chance of saving this one, but it will be a good drill for the pediatric ER staff. We occasionally get adults here. A visitor having chest pain or an actual heart attack. My team needs the experience. This one, though, is probably going to end as just a practice run, training for someone we might actually be able to save in the future. Most people don't come back from a cardiac arrest, even in the hospital.

We assemble in the room, and in the brief moments we have been waiting, my mind wanders back to my first emergency medicine specialty book, given to me as a wedding present by my wife, Marcia. I cherished that book and still have it, probably tucked away in a box. The first chapter was titled "The Mechanisms of Dying," or some such. It is one of the most brilliant inclusions in a book I have ever encountered. The insight of the author was exceptional: If you understand how a person dies, the path for saving the person has been shown. It seems simple: Reverse the mechanisms of dying and save the patient. I often think every ER resident should read this chapter. Sadly, this book has drifted into obscurity, replaced by other more recent texts.

My thoughts vanish as the staff fly through the doors, rolling at breakneck speed down the hall, one person riding the gurney doing CPR. Good CPR, too, I think. Deep chest compressions. Someone paid attention during cardiac lifesaver class. I am thankful I have a good staff made up of good people. As they roll into the room though I have a sinking feeling. This is probably the bluest patient I have ever seen. We call this cyanosis, when the skin turns blue from a lack of oxygenated blood. A color picture of this guy should be in a book, with the simple caption, CYANOSIS.

As the nurses are attaching the defibrillator I listen for breath sounds. He is getting good ventilation with the Ambu bag. Good pulses, too, with CPR, but none on his own. The monitor now comes up and shows ventricular fibrillation, the most serious cardiac rhythm problem because it prevents the heart from pumping blood. Even so, it's better than no heart activity at all. Maybe we can help him after all. But can we really save him? Or has his brain already been too ravaged by the cardiac arrest and lack of oxygen?

We give one amp of epinephrine through his IV and continue CPR for two minutes. This will give his heart time to get increased blood flow and oxygen, improving the odds of our electrical shock actually working. The two minutes seem to drag by but finally we are ready. I know early defibrillation is his only chance. The longer it goes on, the harder it is to reverse. Reverse the mechanisms of dying I think. Save a life, maybe.

The defibrillator is charged up. "Clear," I shout. And boom. The usual convulsive jerk comes with the shock, but he remains in fibrillation. I recharge the defibrillator to the maximum output while the staff restarts CPR. I shout "clear" again, and zap! The tracing line on the EKG suddenly goes flat, and a few seconds later, much to my astonishment, a normal heartbeat appears! I have them continue CPR for a planned two minutes as a heart that has been fibrillating for as long as his does not beat very effectively at first. And then it happens. Something I have never seen before.

Suddenly, and without the slightest warning, my patient, still a ghastly deep blue-purple, sits up in the gurney, his eyes blood shot and bugging out of his head. "Stop what the fuck what you are doing!" he screams. Even I am momentarily taken aback as I am seeing a real-life ghoul yelling right into my face. The nurses and staff fall back several feet from the gurney with their mouths agape. Almost as if he had a machine gun in his hands and just shouted, "I am going to kill you all." It was an astounding moment.

I try to calm him down and regain control of the room and the resuscitation. But he becomes disoriented and combative; I am forced to sedate him. I paralyze and intubate him as well for his own protection. I don't want all of that adrenalin pumping through his system to put him into cardiac fibrillation again.

The EKG confirms a heart attack in progress. His vital signs are good. I have the cardiologist paged STAT at the adult heart center. I start thinking about inducing hypothermia to reduce his core temperature and promote healing. He had a long period of cardiac arrest, his mental status is bad, and although he barely meets criteria for the body-cooling protocol, I give the orders to start it. I have learned if I think about it, I should just do it. The literature is strongly in its favor and I have seen many great saves. Many consultants are still leery of the procedure, and if I leave the decision to them, it likely won't happen. And now I want to pull out all the stops for this patient as I sense a great save in progress.

I decide to ride with him to the next hospital. I am not going to leave his side until he is with the cardiologist. And off we go. Riding in the back of the ambulance is a different experience. You hear the siren loudly and the unit seems to sway side to side in an exaggerated way. Many alterations in our speed along the way, sort of like being on the highway and making a series of sudden stops. After a short ride, the siren goes off, and we pull up to the hospital's ER entrance. The doors open and what the hell? They have taken us to the wrong hospital. So, I give directions again, the doors close, and another ten-minute ride ensues to the correct hospital.

We go directly to the heart cath lab. The cardiologist will check his heart immediately and maybe place a stent to open a closed artery. I stay with my patient until he is actually on the cath table. Ice bags for hypothermia and all. And then the ambulance crew and I take our leave; our contribution to his care is over.

Two days later, I call over to the CCU to check on him. He is still confused but also slowly emerging from hypothermia. He had a major blood vessel blockage in his heart that was successfully stented open. The nurses report the cardiologist is upbeat about his prognosis. Great. I ask the nurse to please give the patient my best when he is awake enough to understand. I am assured that will be done. I'm satisfied, and then I forget about him.

Several days later, I am working the ER again at Children's and I am paged overhead to call the triage desk. I learn that a friend has come to see me. Odd I think, as I am not expecting any friends to visit.

I walk down the long hall and hit the electric panel to open the doors that are right outside of the ER entrance. And there he is. He is wearing a sheepish grin and is clearly uncomfortable being in a hospital and meeting a total stranger. It is my patient! My real-life ghoul. Alive and well. He is here to thank me and the team for saving his life. This happens so rarely that I feel like I am glowing from the inside out. I offer him a brief tour, and we walk down to the resuscitation room. I introduce him to a few of the staff that were there that day. He is kind, thoughtful, and a bit shy to be here with us.

And then I walk him back up to the front and the exit. We shake hands a second time, and he is gone from my life forever. As I head back to the ER, I wonder what he will do with his second chance. I hope he is happy somewhere and still doing well. I wish him a long life.

It was a wonderful morning, Jack. Simply wonderful.

PC

LIKE PUTTING TOOTHPASTE
BACK IN A TUBE

Dear Jack,

These days I am spending roughly half of my shifts in the children's hospital ER. The more serious pediatric emergencies are still delivered into to the main trauma center that we are connected to, serving adults and children. For most of the year, it is a nice change of pace for me to treat kids. Lots of happy endings occur when caring for children, far less chronic illness, and generally more upbeat patients. And I love to joke a bit with the children and make them feel at ease. I've always done at least a third of my shifts on the children's side of the hospital, but this past year it has had more attraction for me. So, I've stepped up my time there. I think I am getting a bit weary of the adults and all of their baggage. You see, the typical kid comes without baggage, doesn't overdose on drugs, has no agendas, and almost always tells you the truth. As I said, it's a refreshing change of pace.

I am sitting, as I often am, charting. Charting, computer order entry, and generating computer discharge instructions are a bigger part of the physician's work load. No longer accomplished by a clerk, these tasks have me tied to the computer for half of each day. I see a nurse hurrying back with a baby in her arms and she calls out to me, "We need you here, Crocker." My nursing staff on the pediatric and adult sides of the ER are very good. They don't panic and they know their stuff. Maybe I should tell them again that

119

I firmly believe that patients in my team's hands have the best chances of a good outcome as any ER in Texas.

I immediately go over to see what the fuss is about. I usually don't get called like this unless a patient is in severe distress, unconscious, or having a cardiac arrest. But the baby is wailing nice and loud, which usually means things aren't too bad. You see, a loudly crying baby tells me the child is awake, has a clear airway, and is breathing well. It most often really means a frightened baby. At any rate, the baby's cry indicates that the ABCs of resuscitation are virtually already complete. Whatever is wrong, I have time. And time is always my friend.

At the bedside, the baby is being placed on a monitor, and the diaper is undone already. And what the fuss is about is immediately obvious. Lying within the diaper is the baby's rectum. Likely pushed out while the baby was straining in an attempt to have a bowel movement. And dude, I mean almost the entire rectum.

Mom, of course, is distraught. "Are you the doctor?" she asks. I answer yes, of course, and she is immediately calmer. No long wait for her baby to be seen. I suspect that possibility crossed her mind while driving in.

This expulsion of the rectum, while not common, is also not rare. It is called rectal prolapse. I have seen this more frequently in elderly adults, and in those cases, it can be a catastrophe. Sometimes there is nothing we can do about it because the patient is too old and infirm to tolerate the surgery. In adults, often without surgery, the rectum simply will not stay in and comes out with each bowel movement. A most uncomfortable situation that will exist the rest of their life. In children, however, the rectum can often be manually put back inside where it belongs. A little inflammation will cause it to scar back in place. Supply a little stool softener, and it may never happen again. The process of healing still astonishes me. How does the body know just what to do? How does it know how much skin to grow back after a burn and when to stop making more? Another of nature's marvels.

After a quick exam to ensure that the expelled rectum has a good blood supply, I place some saline-soaked gauze around it and put the diaper back on. Mom, still a bit pale, looks at me expectantly, and, by her eyes, I know the question is, "what happens next?" I answer before she can ask.

I explain what has happened, giving a brief lecture on rectal prolapse in children. As bad as it looks, it is not a life-or-death emergency, simply an urgent problem. I tell her that I should be able to gently compress the rectum and more or less stuff it all back in. I will call a pediatric surgeon to help me, if needed.

While permits are prepared and signed, I think about this one a bit more. That's more rectum pushed out than I have seen before in a one-year-old. I decide I will call the pediatric surgeon on-call and do the job with him. He is a great friend. It's also our favorite lunch offering today--fried shrimp in the doctor's dining room--so we can eat together when we're done. Often, whichever one of us arrives to find a surprise fried shrimp day, pages the other. If our work allows, we head right down for lunch. Having him help with this baby is a good idea, regardless. He's a great doc with dexterous hands. This will be a challenge, like pushing toothpaste back into a tube. What I mean is, when the rectum comes out, it also usually comes out "inside-out," making it even more difficult to slide back into place. I also order a little morphine for the baby. Enough I hope to provide just a little mild sedation and take the edge off. Every time the baby yells or cries, it increases the intra-abdominal pressure, and this will work against us. A full sedation isn't usually necessary, though, it could be a helpful convenience for us. But first, do no harm. No convenience sedation by me. Even a simple sedation can turn sour, so for now, I'm holding off on it.

Gloved and gowned up, we begin. My friend's hands nearest the patient slowly compressing the mass and attempting to slide it forward back inside. I am at the further end doing the same thing. Gentle compression, gently pushing. There is just enough room for both our hands working together. We get two inches back in, and an inch juts back out. Back and forth we go, making a little progress at a time. As we get to the final two inches we just can't get that last part tucked back in. Our fingers work together but the bowel fights back, popping back out around our fingers in every direction except back in. The bowel has now become swollen, and pushing it back through the small opening where it must go seems impossible. We have an idea. I hold the mass in place and my friend uses Q-tips to tuck the final swollen edges back inside. We make some progress. And then whoosh, all of a sudden, the last of the rectum vanishes, seemingly sucked back inside the baby where it belongs. Relief. We are both sweating lightly now, and Mom looks relieved. Her baby is back to normal. And that's how you put a rectum back where it belongs.

While you and I were back taking Chem 1A together, I never dreamed I would actually be doing this kind of stuff. I wish my Dad were still alive as he would have been both amazed and proud. I think intimidated a bit, too, considering his little kid is now part of a team that takes care of the worst kind of emergencies. He would understand that there is no magic that saves lives in an ER, just regular people doing their jobs. Or, perhaps he would shudder, I chuckle to myself. My kid's in charge of what? Once I became an adult, I realized you'll always be just their little kid. Dad will always remember me as the 12-year-old pitcher who was afraid to let his fastball fly on a three and two count.

I get a fresh diaper and start to put it on. But it's some newer kind of diaper, and I just can't tell the front from the back or how to secure it. My friend laughs and takes over, as can be his way, but thirty seconds later, he also is stymied. Neither of us has diapered a baby in ages, and, well, they don't make them like they used to. Mom steps up, and in three seconds, the diaper is on. We all laugh. I look at Mom and all I can offer is, "With over sixty years of clinical experience between us, we can put your baby's rectum back in place, but we can't change a diaper." My friend and I are obviously in need of grandchildren. We give instructions for follow-up care and say our goodbyes.

As I walk down toward the doctor's dining room I consider my career. It feels like I was made for this job. Not "made" in terms of molded by education and training for it. Rather "born" for it. I have truly found my dream job and love every minute of it. I feel lucky when I think of so many people who hate their job. Mine seems to grow more fulfilling every year. I am one lucky guy, I tell myself as I shuffle down the hall, and, man, do those fried shrimp smell good.

PC

A SWOLLEN TONGUE, A BRUSH WITH DEATH

Dear Jack,

Yesterday I worked the 3 p.m. to 1 a.m. shift. You can always count on this one being pretty busy. As I walked up to the ER from under the helipad where I park my car, I see a mess unfolding. Five EMS units in the ambulance arrival area were in various stages of unloading patients or restocking. People were milling about. I walked past them, came in the front entrance, and saw a packed waiting room. It's loud, too. Eyes stare at me as I walk in wearing scrubs, and I don't see any friendly faces. People probably have been waiting a few hours and now they're getting fed up.

After I drop my stuff at the doc's work area, I hunt up the charge nurse for a report. She's one of my favorites, and I have worked with her in the ER since I was an intern. I get a quick hug and a muffled, "Glad you're here." And then she adds, "Now go to work." She is a no-nonsense type and has no time at that moment for even a quick report. She's a born Texan and was raised like one.

Most of what I need to know is contained in the chart rack, which stands in the main treatment area. They wait for one of us doctors to pick them up. Usually, the charts are sorted by the triage nurse, first by severity, then by arrival time. The ER charge nurse will check them periodically and re-sort them, as necessary. This is an essential step as patient conditions can change and triage errors occur. Re-sorting improves patient safety. But it can really anger the patients with minor problems who keep getting bumped to the end of the line. Today, the rack is double stacked. I estimate that thirty-five charts are in the stack, all patients waiting to be seen. I am going to be busy the entire shift just trying to catch up.

I decide to quickly go through the charts myself before I pick one up. Maybe I can chip away at the backup by getting an X-ray or some lab work started. And maybe someone just sitting there has to be seen now. No matter how careful you and the staff are, disasters can and do happen. You do not want to be surprised by a cardiac arrest in the waiting room, I assure you.

As I look through the charts, one about ten slots from the front catches my attention. A woman in her late sixties is waiting with a chief complaint of "tongue swelling." I look around thinking I will ask one of the nurses to go check on her, but everyone is busy. The ER can look like chaos to outsiders, but everyone is actually working diligently, either carrying out a doctor's orders or rechecking patients. If you have a good crew, it runs like a well-oiled machine. I just take the chart and go out to the waiting room myself.

Waiting rooms can be hazardous for patients. Every busy hospital has had their share of disasters. The most feared is the sleeping patient who has been waiting for hours with some seemingly innocuous complaint. And, of course, when their name is called, no one answers. They aren't sleeping after all. They are dead.

When I call out this woman's name, two younger women wave me over. They have brought in their mother. As I make my way through the crowd, it looks like mom is in no real distress. I say hello and introduce myself. As I look more closely at her, it is obvious things are not normal. Her tongue is badly swollen, maybe an inch and a half thick, and protruding a bit out of her mouth. I ask if she is on blood pressure medicines, expecting I know the answer. Sure enough, I hear the word I expect and dread. Lisinopril. Damn. This one should have been brought to the treatment area immediately.

Some medications can cause a rather odd condition called angioedema. It usually occurs during the first couple of months after the medicine is started but can happen at any time. Not really an allergic reaction but a side effect as the drug interferes with normal deactivation of immune system mediators. In some cases, the swelling can be rapidly progressive and life-threatening when it involves the tongue or the floor of the mouth. ER doc horror stories abound around this one because the usual treatments for a true allergic angioedema simply do not work. Adrenalin, antihistamines, and steroids are a waste of time. The patient worsens while you try the usual things and if you delay too long the problem becomes critical. The airway gets so blocked you can no longer get a breathing tube down. Patients die of suffocation, right before your eyes.

So, I grab a wheelchair and we start rolling back to the crash area. I ask the staff to make room for her. Move someone else less serious out into the hall.

I can now take some time for a better history and exam. The swelling started after her morning dose of medicine that was taken late, only a few hours ago. This has never happened before. It has been slowly getting worse. The daughters are concerned. It is painless and this rather stoic mom is not bothered much by it. Her voice is muffled in what we term a hot potato voice and this possibly indicates swelling lower in her airway too. Not a good sign. I enter her orders and get the nurses attention to get started on them despite being busy elsewhere. And, yes, I do order the same bullshit, worthless treatment with adrenalin, antihistamines, and steroids. The reason to do this is that there is a small chance that this is the more reversible form of allergic angioedema caused by something else. I have to try them while we observe her closely. I ask for a crash cart to be brought to the bedside.

I am hoping that, given we are a few hours into this problem, perhaps it won't progress. But if it does, that can be an airway nightmare. I will keep a close eye on her.

I'm back at the bedside in perhaps just fifteen minutes. I'll see if she is actually responding to the meds I have ordered. Damn, she is clearly worsening, and rapidly. Her tongue is now two inches thick and protruding about two inches from her mouth. She's in no real distress, but the time to act has come. And I am afraid it won't be easy.

I explain the situation to mom and her daughters. Their concerns and mine have gone from the yellow zone to red. I see the alarm on their faces. If I looked in the mirror I could probably see it on my own face. I tell them that I need to sedate her and place an endotracheal tube down into her windpipe so that she can breathe as in minutes her airway will be swollen closed. There is no other reasonable option. The daughters agree to move forward. Mom, however, is not sold. She is, after all, awake and alert and can make her own treatment decisions under the law. Even if they are, simply put, stupid, and born of fright.

This is an ER doc's nightmare in progress. The patient may be dying and simply doesn't recognize it. Or believe it. I am a stranger to their mom and suggesting drastic measures. Her own beloved doctor says this medicine is good for her. I will explain again and agree normally this medication is great treatment for blood pressure but sometimes this side effect happens. Maybe if I acknowledge her doctor is a wonderful guy, which he likely is, it will build some needed trust in me, the stranger. We again review airway obstruction and suffocation. The daughters agree to move forward. Mom remains recalcitrant.

I ask the ER tech to also bring over the emergency cricothyrotomy set up. This is to perform what is often termed a tracheostomy. We simply make a surgical incision in the neck just below the larynx and insert a tube through the hole securing airflow to the lungs. Sounds deceptively simple, and in most adult patients, it's not particularly difficult. Intimidating, yes. In this case, I am not anxious to perform this procedure, and certainly not while she is crashing with an airway obstruction. She is short and obese. A very short neck I think, which will make the procedure harder. I palpate her larynx and the landmarks I need to guide me can barely be felt. I am now stuck in this nightmare.

She continues to progress, and I now have no choice but to act or watch her die by suffocation. I ask her if she wants to die? She says "No." I explain the situation again. No, she does not want a tube down her throat. Jesus Fucking Christ!! I simply have failed to convince her. The daughters are sold, but their mom is competent to make her own decisions, and that legally binds me. I can strictly follow her statement and likely watch her die, but I can't do that. I can go against her wishes and save her life but may face a horrible ethics review. Or even worse, I can go against he wishes, paralyze her, and then be unable to establish an airway. And then I will have murdered her. I am between a rock and a hard place. I decide I will accept her "I'm not ready to die" as a consent and decide to proceed. I just can't do otherwise and would rather defend myself later against proceeding without consent versus a wrongful death suit or watching her suffocate before my eyes. I feel like primum non nocere demands that I act, consent be damned.

A swollen partially obstructed airway is one of the worst emergencies we can face. These are difficult decisions and high-risk for everyone. So, I am very, very careful. I have a little latitude, for the moment, and get HurriCaine spray to numb her throat. I ask the respiratory techs to be paged STAT and set up the ventilator. I get a mild sedative and the equipment to intubate. The nurse readies a stronger dose of sedative to be followed by paralytic drugs once the tube is in and her airway secured.

Have you ever seen "Ferris Bueller's Day Off?" I think of his description of his friend Cameron being wired tight all of the time. "His anus is so tight that if you stuck a piece of coal up his ass it would be a diamond the next day," Ferris said. That's my ass right now. If I had a piece of coal right now, I could make a diamond and retire tomorrow.

After numbing her throat with the spray, I carefully advance the laryngoscope with her fully awake. The cricothyrotomy tray is ready. Drugs are ready. The anesthesiologist is taking care of a critical case, so it is just going to have to be me alone. Mom remains oblivious. I let the daughters stay with her to hold her hand. I am long past being bothered by families in the room while I do a procedure. The HurriCaine spray to numb her mouth and throat has worked wonderfully, and I can see the mess I am facing better. I can still see her vocal cords, maybe half the view I normally get. Everything is very swollen, but I am ninety-nine percent sure I can get her intubated. That beats the hell out of trying to cut an airway into her neck. But because I don't have her consent, I am on the thinnest of ice, and it is audibly cracking. My patient and I could plunge into icy waters in the next few moments.

I look at the daughters, and they nod. Do what you need to do to save Mom, doc. This is really the worst situation I face at work. An actively swelling airway obstruction in a patient with a short, fat neck who would rather wait and see. But it is now or never. Everything is ready. A little sedative is given, and in I go. It's a relatively easy intubation, with the breathing tube going right down into the trachea. She struggles a bit and coughs. The nurse pushes the rest of the drugs in. Within thirty seconds, she is quietly sleeping, her airway secure.

I am so relieved I forget about hunting for that piece of coal. That diamond though would have been nice. Inside I am celebrating. Jumping up and down with joy. I do wonder just how badly the docs who take over her care will criticize me. What kind of peer review will I face? Fuck it. I saved her life, and I know it.

She is taken away to the ICU. Her daughters are so thankful that they hug me. Usually, at this point, the patient and family are out of my life forever. Not this time.

About two hours later, I get a call from an ICU nurse. The ICU attending wants me to come over to the ICU. No doubt, this is the dressing down I expected. What were you thinking? I'll be asked. That was dangerous. You are just a stupid cowboy ER doc. Oh, well. Like I said, fuck it.

I walk over to the attending, trying not to feel sullen. I know what I did was right. He flashes a brief smile. A good sign. He says, "Go take a look at your patient now." I move into her room and am dumbfounded. Her whole face is swollen now. Her lips three inches thick. Her tongue now looks like some hideous cartoon character. It is hanging down below her chin. The airway tube I put in now seems to be coming out of the center of a melon. Without it, she would be dead.

I return to the ER and finish my shift. About 1:30 a.m., I say goodbye to the charge nurse. She says, "Go get some sleep. I am glad you were here today." I live for such moments. Despite the hour and after a long shift, I feel absolutely great, not even tired.

As I walk outside and down to my car, I am planning on a treat. A late-night snack of hot wings and a cold beer. Not regular hot wings. Atomic hot wings! I'm thinking a double order.

Today, I feel I have earned them.

PC

P.S. On the way home I listened to Baba O'Riley by The Who. At the very first verse Roger Daltry sums it up. Speaking his thoughts regarding forgiveness or the need to prove your right if what you have done is "right" for you. It's just how I am feeling.

I BECOME A PATIENT

Dear Jack,

I'm working a busy night shift in the pediatric ER, and just after 1 a.m., it is slowing down a bit. As I come up for air, I suddenly realize I feel bad. I have a headache, something I rarely suffer, and it's a monster. Throbbing and unrelenting. Even the skin on my head hurts. I take my temperature and it's 103.8.

It's flu season, but I am dutiful about getting my annual shot. I've had several pediatric shifts lately, and kids, especially under age five, will just cough snot right in your face. Then smile at you. Oblivious to the fact they may have just infected you with their disease. So, I always make sure I am immunized. Even so, no shot is a hundred percent perfect, and, now, I'm afraid I am coming down with the flu. I stick it out another hour or so, though I am simply miserable. Fortunately, we have three other doctors in the ER tonight, so I beg off the rest of my shift. I've never called in sick or left a shift early, but there's a first time for everything. I simply will be useless between now and 4 a.m., when I am supposed to get off. I accept the inevitable good-natured teasing about being a wimp.

Driving home, I'm feeling worse by the minute. As soon as I arrive, I down 800 milligrams of ibuprofen and a glass of water. I climb into bed. I hope to feel a little sore throat, a cough, maybe some sniffles, as they will likely confirm my suspicions of flu and ease my worry of meningitis. It strikes

131

me funny to be hoping for flu symptoms. But meningitis can be even less fun. I note that my neck isn't stiff and that I have no increased pain with flexion. Probably not meningitis. But I know I don't want to go back to the hospital and have someone do a spinal tap to see what may be causing producing my misery. Period. I slowly fall into a fitful sleep.

Morning comes, and, maybe, the headache is a little better, maybe. I conclude that if it is meningitis, it is the less serious viral variety, and I will just tough it out at home. I have a few days off anyway. My fever is 102.6, so I swallow more ibuprofen and head for the couch. Every muscle and bone seem to ache. OK, I guess it is the flu after all.

I don't believe most doctors make good patients. I make up my mind to try to be a good one and not call my own primary care physician until he is needed. On day four of continuous fever, never less than 102.6, I decide it's time to make that call. I had gone hog hunting in South Texas a week before and am growing a bit concerned about Rickettsial disease, bacterial infections spread by arthropods, likes fleas, ticks, and lice. I still lack any flu symptoms so I call my doctor and discuss my concerns. He attempts to reassure me I just have the flu. After some cajoling, he relents and orders some titers. These tests are being done to see if I have any acute antibodies to one of the uncommon febrile diseases. Go home, he says. Rest. Drink plenty of water.

Two days pass, and I notice I am short of breath climbing the stairs to reach my home office. I tell myself I am simply tired and feverish. After each half flight on my way up, I pant, and then pant some more at my desk. I decide to call my doctor again. A chest X-ray shows only what appear to be some viral changes, small infiltrates in my lungs. No pneumonia. Go home, he says again. Rest. Drink plenty of water. I go down the hall to a friend who is an infectious disease specialist. He also thinks I have the flu. Go home, he says. Rest. Drink plenty of water.

On day eight of this continuous fever, I am growing more concerned. I get another chest X-ray that shows some small fluid collections at the base of my lungs. My partners bring me some Levaquin (an antibiotic) samples, and I will see the pulmonologist in the morning. He similarly is not impressed and tells me to go home. Rest. Drink plenty of water. It's probably a virus, but he tells me to continue the Levaquin, just in case. Always hedge your bets.

I go home and begin scanning the Internet. I am convinced I have spotless Rocky Mountain Fever or Typhus. Both occur in Texas, but they are fairly rare, particularly Typhus. I start some Internet chats with a few university infectious disease specialists with a special interest in typhus. I feel like crap. I haven't eaten anything since this started.

On day nine, I call my doctor and ask him to meet me in the ER. I sign in. I'm done with being "a good patient" and order every test I think is relevant. My wife, daughter, and two of my partners all ask me if I am dying. I say I don't think so. Maybe it's endocarditis, an inflammation of the heart and its valves, one friend one offers. Great, just what I need. And he has a good point. I've ordered blood cultures already, four sets of them, so we will see. I want relief. My blood count is low, my platelet count is low, and my sodium is low. My serum protein is dropping. Everything else is normal. This sounds like typhus to me, but I get no other takers. Wait for the blood cultures, they say. For now, go home, blah-blah, blah-blah.

On day ten, I decide I am going to start doxycycline. Break some rules and act as my own doctor. One of the Internet doctors who specializes in typhus agrees. I review it with a local pediatric infectious disease specialist, and she thinks it is a good idea too. Time to start getting better. I take two capsules and head back to the couch, my home for almost two weeks. A number of hours later, my fever spikes to 105.8. Holy crap! I am home alone and this is truly a dangerously high fever. I wonder if I should call someone to sit me with in case it climbs higher and incapacitates me. Nah, I'm not going to bother anyone. At this point, I feel so awful that dying actually doesn't sound all that horrible.

I presume the increased fever is the result of what's called the Jarisch-Herxheimer reaction. It is believed to be a result of the bacteria dying in response to the antibiotic. Good. I'm a bit nervous, but I try to fall asleep after more ibuprofen plus Tylenol. I reassure myself: Tomorrow I will be better.

But day twelve arrives, and while the fever has gone down a bit I still don't feel like eating. Some chicken broth is about all I can stomach. The phone rings, and it's my doctor. "Has anyone called you yet?" he asks. "No," I say. "Why?" He tells me all of my blood cultures are growing strep milleri, a potentially virulent pathogen that can be life-threatening. "Come to the hospital now and get admitted," he says. "I will call in your orders." I cry briefly. I do not want to be this sick or go to the hospital. We pack up and go anyway. I'm feeling about as down as I have ever felt.

As a physician, I am acutely aware of the risks of being a hospitalized patient. You face the possibility of hospital-acquired infections, the kinds that resist many or all antibiotics. On top of that, there are blood clots, pulmonary embolism, and medical errors to worry about. By any definition, I have been septic with bacteria running free in my bloodstream for almost two weeks, and now I fear a brain abscess. I'm scared.

At the hospital, I weigh in at 149 pounds! Just two weeks ago, I was 175. I look and feel like a dead man walking. I spend the next two days being scanned from head to toe. I get dental X-rays; contrasted CT scans of my brain, chest, and abdomen; an echocardiogram; an upper and lower endoscopy; and a central venous catheter. Oh yeah, and I can't forget all of the needle biopsies into my liver. They want samples of the pus pockets and finally believe I am sick.

The staff doctors who are my friends are nothing short of wonderful to me. The best doctors of each department come in to oversee my procedures and interpret the studies. I remember to personally thank each one during my recovery. All of this is happening on a holiday weekend. They come in anyway. Nice.

One unfortunate necessity of all these procedures is sequential sedations, or anesthesia. And, of course, the colon prep. I still haven't eaten, but I am not hungry anyway.

A few hours later, after my very first dose of ceftriaxone, I feel like a miracle has occurred. I wake up at 2 a.m., and the fever is gone! I actually feel good. Hungry and tired, but good.

At this point, I have been sick for over two full weeks. They have found the multiple abscesses in my liver are also growing strep milleri, a gut bacteria. I argue to continue the doxycycline, as well as the ceftriaxone. Always hedge your bets. They relent. Before I am discharged the infectious disease doctor comes by and says "Good news, we have found the cause. You have ehrlichiosis." It's a bacterial disease spread by the bite of an infected tick. Like typhus and Rocky Mountain Spotted Fever, it is an unusual intra-cellular organism. These organisms break down your cell membranes and can allow gut bacteria to enter your blood stream. It all seems to make sense. I go home on IV ceftriaxone and doxycycline. The treatment plan is for eight weeks of antibiotics. I weigh out of the hospital at 147 pounds. I have lost almost thirty pounds.

I return to the hospital after a week of antibiotics to have the abscess that developed in my liver drained under CT scan guidance. I'm not looking forward to this. More needles in my liver is zero fun. I get into the scanner, IV contrast goes in, and I wait. But lo and behold, and to everyone's amazement, they are gone in just a week's time! There is nothing to drain. My liver is doing yeoman's work regenerating itself and healing the abscesses.

I actually feel pretty good. I am still short of breath because my red blood cell count is down to twenty-two percent, roughly half of what it is supposed to be. I am voracious and loving every bit of food I can consume. Breakfast is a McDonald's Big Breakfast every morning at 7 a.m. At 10, I drink a protein shake with a banana, milk, and some nuts. Lunch is at 1 p.m. and is a double Wendy's cheeseburger with fries. Dinners are even bigger. Piles of pasta and meatballs. Whole rotisserie chickens. Grilled steak. I eat like a pig. My bedtime snack is a whole package of either Pepperidge Farm apple turnovers or an entire package of Sister Sara's cinnamon rolls. I am probably consuming 6,000 calories a day. I eat like this for over a month and finally hit 180 pounds. I'm feeling like my old self. Plus five pounds.

At my one month follow-up, my doctor comes in looking very contrite. He, and he alone, apologizes for letting me get so sick before acting. None of the other specialists seem to care they missed the disease. The comment "interesting" is about all I hear. Interesting is the last thing you want to be to a doctor. Interesting cases suck for the patient.

I'm allowed to return to administrative work after two weeks at home and to clinical work in a month. I felt ready after a week of antibiotics, but I will wait as directed. IV antibiotics at home are continued for eight weeks and then continued two more weeks for good measure. The central venous catheter finally comes out at fourteen weeks. I survived, with no complications. Hallelujah.

I learned many things from this experience that will help me later in practice. I always thought I was an above-average patient listener. I learned to listen better. Sometimes, the patient is right. When I give a diagnosis now and the patient pushes back, I rethink the entire case. Start to finish. Am I missing something? I may or may not order some tests to rule out something more serious, but I always give their concerns new and serious considerations. I offer to see them the next day. And if my concern is high and I am unlikely to see them again, they get my home phone number. Call if you need me or you are worse and your doctor can't see you.

Unexplained febrile illnesses are now my most interesting cases. It's even more interesting if the person traveled. I am now very well-versed on these diseases and love to be the one to suggest the diagnosis to my partners when asked. I'm enjoying being a bit of a know-it-all in this narrow spectrum of medicine.

Over coffee a month later, I tell my still contrite and apologetic doctor to forget about it. I am well. No harm, no foul. But he can learn from this, as I have. Listen to patients. It takes patience, but, sometimes, they are right.

End of story? Not quite. My eight-week antibody titers finally return, and much to my satisfaction, the results confirm my Typhus titers have risen significantly. There were only four confirmed cases in Texas this year. A pretty rare diagnosis. It is also confirmed I have had ehrlichiosis at some time in my past. My infectious disease doctor advises me to spend more time at the mall and less time in the woods. Sorry, doc, I prefer the woods.

PC

A BAD SHIFT

Dear Jack,

This shift began like so many others. I am third in line at the hospital dining room omelet station. Its 7:01 a.m., and the chow line opened one minute ago. I always come to work about fifteen minutes early, take report from the off-going doctor, and then, if there are no patients who need to be seen, I head here. The omelets are ridiculous: two tablespoons of butter, four eggs, sausage, spinach, onions, jalapenos, and tomatoes. I always ask to hold the cheese, but he always gives it to me anyway. A couple of quick scoops of fresh made jalapeno salsa, and I'm on my way back to the ER.

I don't like to get up, shave, shower and hop right into the truck and head for the hospital. I like to take my time in the morning. So, morning starts at 4:45 a.m. I spend a few moments greeting my dog, and then I start the coffee. One of the best presents I ever got was a coffee grinder from my daughter. Fresh ground coffee beans every morning. It really makes a difference. I will mix half French roast and half medium roast beans, to cut the bitter edge. While it's brewing, I take the dog out to do his business and play for a few minutes. Then turn on CNN's HLN and sit back for a bit the news. The haze of a night's sleep slowly lifts as I enjoy my coffee.

I return to the ER and sat down at my station. My omelet smells delicious and I can't wait to dig into it. I see a new chart in the rack and am tempted to just eat quickly and then see what's up as nobody has come to me with any concerns. Likely, it's the chart of a routine patient. But duty calls, and I can't eat until I see the patient. It is why I am here. I am not here for the hot breakfast. So, I grab the chart and head to his room.

I know in an instant this case will be a tough one. I momentarily silently curse the nurses who have not paged me to see this patient immediately. Their complacency aggravates me sometimes. A man in his mid 50s or so is sweating profusely with a heart rate of 136. What bothers me most is what's called his QRS on the heart monitor. The QRS is a squiggle segment in the middle of a heartbeat that shows how the heart is transmitting electrical signals through its conduction system. His measure is wide, frighteningly wide. Despite my years of experience, this is precisely the kind of case that I dread, the most fear-invoking, the patient with a wide QRS tachycardia. He is awake and alert. I learn the episode began almost eight hours ago, complete with chest pressure, palpitations, sweating, and shortness of breath. He elected to stay at home till morning. He hates hospitals and doctors are not far behind. I understand completely.

He will need a quick EKG to verify what I'm seeing on the monitor. It confirms my fears: A QRS of 0.16. That is way too wide. It spells a sick heart and a failing cardiac conduction system. In capital letters. His blood pressure is a little too low, and I order a quick infusion of fluid and explain the situation to him. He's afraid, especially when I tell him we may need to shock his heart to restore a normal rhythm. Again, I understand his fear.

My first impulse is to use a very old drug, a time-honored standby for this heart rhythm problem, called procainamide. The other option is immediate electrical cardioversion, just what he fears most. I choose to temporize for the moment, give the fluids, increase his blood pressure a bit, contact the cardiologist on call, and review his past medical record quickly. Patients often seem to have no idea of how severe their actual, lurking health problems are. One tool that computerized medical records has given us is the ability to obtain a patient's past history in seconds. I open my patient's chart as I await a call back from the cardiologist.

Things unfortunately are worse than I thought. My patient's baseline measurement of the amount of blood that gets squeezed out with each beat, called the ejection fraction, is only twenty-four percent. It should be closer to fifty percent or higher. His is a sick heart, all right. I don't know whether it's bad from a previous heart attack or the wear-and-tear phenomena termed ischemic cardiomyopathy. I am frankly more concerned with this patient right now than with any patient suffering a full cardiac arrest. I know in that situation, the cat is already out of the bag. We have clear guidelines to follow after a cardiac arrest. In this case, my goal is to keep the cat in the bag, stabilize him, and PREVENT a cardiac arrest. This is far harder to accomplish than simply running a code.

I recheck him and am slightly relieved to find his blood pressure is up a bit, heart rate down a little, and he feels slightly better. Still sweating, or diaphoretic, as we say, but this also has improved. Things may not go so badly after all. I seem to have a little more time to figure things out and hear back from my consultant.

I have sent the EKG by wire to the cardiologist who calls me back. We discuss the case. I would very much like for him to be here right now, but he is over an hour away in another city. And he is all I have for backup. He is comfortable with my approach for the moment. He suggests amiodarone, a drug I do not like. All heart medications for rhythm control are also cardiac poisons, of sorts. It is how they work. Poison just part of the heart's electrical conduction system, and the problem can be solved. Too much medication poisons the entire heart. And the risk of this is higher with an already sick heart. As the patient has improved a bit, we agree to temporize a bit longer, continue fluids, move the patient to a procedure room, and cautiously give the drug rather than use the electrical shock he fears. I make my case again for procainamide, but I am told amiodarone is the safest and best choice. Just do it. And, so it goes.

As I give the orders, which will take a few minutes, I discover my omelet is cold. The butter congealed. Maybe later I will get back to it. Five more patients are now waiting to be seen. I start bouncing around, seeing others, getting their evaluation and treatments ordered.

Back to my most pressing case, I wonder: Why does it take so much time to get this drug? Why isn't this life-saving medication even stocked in the emergency department? It is available for cardiac arrests but not for more routine infusions in which the pharmacist has time to the check the dose and prepare the drip. This waiting is a waste of precious time, as far as I'm concerned.

The nurse comes over to the area where I am charting and tells me my patient's blood pressure has now dropped to seventy. I head straight over and find the infusion has already run in. "What?" I think. I ask her exactly when the drug was started as it is supposed to be a twenty-to-thirty-minute infusion. She has no answer. I wonder if the drug may have been given a bit too rapidly for his sick heart to tolerate. Perhaps this choice of drug is suppressing his heart muscle excessively. Or that the combination of the medication with his sick exhausted heart was just too much. I am furious but keep it to myself. I simply must deal with the situation as it now exists. You must always keep your cool in critical situations. Panic, anger… both are contagious and lead to bad care and more mistakes.

I have no choice now. I page the cardiologist STAT and start preparing for an electrical cardioversion. Things simply are going downhill no matter what I do. I sedate him moderately and deliver the shock. It takes two in increasing shocks before it works. He is successfully cardioverted to a normal electrical rhythm but has no pulse. Shit. His already weak heart is likely stunned by the combination of the electrical shock and medications. We start CPR. I see his wife outside the room clutching her face. Pure and simple grief. I am so sorry for her. After about ten minutes of CPR and intravenous epinephrine, we get a pulse and a blood pressure. He is combative, screaming and pulling out his IVs. I use the drug succinylcholine to paralyze him and then intubate and place him on a ventilator. I am devastated by this turn of events. My bad feelings from the start have all come to pass.

I consult for helicopter transfer to the nearest specialized heart center, which is about an hour-and-a-half away by car. I suggest hypothermia treatment but am advised to wait. The sooner, the better, I argue. He is still unstable and perhaps we should wait. I know what the literature says and prefer hypothermia as soon as possible. But I agree to wait.

Now to the bad news room. I hate going in there. It is an opportunity to explain the situation to the family, offer what comfort is possible, but I have to tell it straight. The prognosis is not good. I am worried about anoxic brain damage. That he was semi-awake and purposeful is the only bright spot I can offer. His pulse oxygen concentrations remained good throughout CPR, I say, but I know his heart was in a very low output state. I have seen the transient brain effects of anoxia and they sometimes get better in two or three days. Not this time, I fear. Despite this disaster, his wife thanks me for my help and starts the drive to the transfer center. I am saddened by her thanks and devastated at this outcome.

The cardiologist finally arrives and reviews the case. He attempts to console me. "You did everything right," he tells me. "It is what I would have done if I were here. He had a sick heart and sick hearts die." His words are wasted on me.

I'm so miserable I feel like going home. A failed therapy at my hands. Never before have I seen every single thing I attempted to help a patient go sour in such devastating sequence. Sure, we have complications, a simple case that goes south, and then back again. But never like this. I have only had two patients actually die while under my direct care. I am unfamiliar with this situation and state of mind. Miserable and defeated hardly describe it. My omelet goes in the trash. The shift continues, as it must.

I will always wonder how the case would have gone if I had just done the things that I preferred for therapy. Listened to my own gut on the medication and the body cooling. Would it have been different if I had had no other patients in the ER or a second doctor to take care of them while I focused only on him? Would things have gone better if I had stood at the bedside throughout his care, supervising every step? Would he and his family still be intact? He died a week later.

I want to speak with his widow desperately. Explain his condition in detail, every step we took trying to save him and why, and how everything was stacked against us. In a fashion that we didn't have time for that horrible day. I believe it will help her grieving. And I feel she should know. But there is no opportunity. I'm despondent for weeks after this one.

Could I have saved him? Or was fate in the driver's seat? Maybe it was just his time.

PC

FUN WITH THE "NEW GUY"

Dear Jack,

    While I sit sipping coffee at the desk waiting for my next patient, it strikes me the ER is a very special place. Imagine there is a group of people just waiting to try to care for whatever disaster has befallen them. No holds barred; bring us anything. We've got you covered, 24/7/365, whether you're choking on a bite of dinner, having a heart attack, vomiting blood, or bleeding profusely from having your arm torn off in a horrible accident.

    I can tell you without hesitation that the people who work here are special and will do whatever they can to help. There are no real classes in how to care for a torn-off arm, but we will deal with it. And these life-threatening situations, many without guideposts for treatment, build a camaraderie that is unique. It's a lot like military combat teams. Standing side by side almost daily, sometimes for years, builds special friendships. Those of us who have done it for many years consider each other our extended family. We spend as much of our waking lives together as we spend with our own family at home, maybe more.

    There also are no classes on how to care for yourself and cope with what can be a stress- and grief-filled career. Most of us feel some stress and tension with the difficult cases, especially when we imagine a loved one—or ourselves—lying on that gurney.

All of that stress requires a way to release the tension. The gallows humor of the ER staff is infamous. One frequent target is "the new guy or gal." At some point during your initiation, you should expect some humorous prank. At your expense, of course.

Imagine it's 1 a.m. during a grueling shift, with twenty-five charts piled up on the rack. We are all tired and need some relief. The NG, the new guy in this case, is still in that initial phase of horror, terror, and shock, witnessing what we sometimes need to do. NG will get used to it. We all do. NG will learn to function under frightening circumstances. So, it's time for lesson one. We are in a GYN room with the door closed. My nurse cracks it open and says, "Hey, NG, we have a bleeder in here, and you need to run down stairs to central supply right now. Doc needs a set of STERILE FALLOPIAN TUBES right now! Run, she's bleeding!" NG doesn't even know for sure where the supply room is. The hospital's lower level is a maze. I am sure his tension during his essential quest for sterile fallopian tubes is high, and rising. NG finds the supply room, but the night staff cannot locate these life-saving tubes. This item is simply not on the computer list. NG runs back, knocks on the door, and the nurse answers, "What?? They can't find them? Those idiots. Tell them to look under 'tubes, sterile, Fallopian.' Hurry. we need those damn tubes." And off he goes to set those idiots downstairs straight on how to enter the computer request enabling him to retrieve them before the patient bleeds out. NG does his best, the stress ever-mounting.

Ultimately, NG realizes there are no such items. He's been had. He finally recalls from a high school health class that the tubes he seeks are simply the medical term for the canal that carries the human egg from the ovary to the uterus. NG returns red-faced, frustrated, and humiliated. We, however, think it is hilarious. Some of the stress of the shift is relieved, and we can continue. NG will learn. In a year or two, NG will pull the same trick on the next NG.

Another middle of the night favorite for NG is to send him to the waiting room to find a patient. The frustrated nurse finds NG, hands him a chart, and says, "This patient is not answering the overhead pages. Go out to the waiting room and just try walking around asking for him." NG dutifully goes out in search of the patient. Chart in hand, he sees that the patient's name is Jack Mehoff. We can hear him through the ER entry doors yelling for Jack Mehoff. We are in hysterics. He returns to report nobody is answering. The nurse suggests he go back out there and go from patient to patient, asking, 'Are you Mr. Jack Mehoff?" I simply can't stay away from the spectacle, so I go out to the police officers' one-way window into the waiting room to watch. We are simply dying of laughter. Even the waiting patients, despite their long wait and frustration, are starting to look around with bemused smiles. Does this guy really think there's a Mr. Jack Mehoff among them? He finally gives up realizing he has been had. Victim of a phony name with a double meaning. Sorry, NG. We simply needed a break.

On rare occasions, the ER will empty of patients around 4 a.m. After working most of the night, you would think the staff would be happy to just sit around and chill. Not a chance. Before too long, mischief creeps into their heads, and another joke is born. This one will be on the incoming morning doctor.

They gather up about fifteen fake charts and stack them on the "to be seen" rack. Then they close all the curtains around the ER gurneys, making the place look packed with patients. A lookout is posted to watch for the doc arriving from the parking area. The staff begins to shuffle around, talk loudly, and do their best to look busy. All the time waiting to see the look on the doctor's face when he or she realizes they have walked into a disaster. They look up and shake their heads. "Going to be a bad one doc, sorry. We just got slammed." The doc is crestfallen, bracing for a bitch of a morning. Cleaning up last night's mess and no breakfast, to boot. The doc may even become angry and slam the charts down on the desk, cursing the night doc for not keeping up. Finally, the doc gets up to take the first chart and prepares to deal with the crappy poker hand that's been dealt. Chart in hand, the doc goes into the first room, and no patient. Patients do go wandering, and this will require extra work and time. "Where is the patient that's supposed to be in room twelve?" the doc shouts. The same routine happens with the next patient, and then the staff, now assembled at the desk watching, simply breaks into laughter. Fooled you, doc.

We all work holidays; it's part of the job. Emergencies don't take the day off to celebrate, and neither do we. But we do what we can to take the edge off of working when the world is watching football and stuffing themselves. We do our best to replicate it. Everyone brings in a covered dish. Someone will cook a turkey. There will be fried chicken and tons of food. We will take turns eating and sharing another holiday away from our families. We have to make our own fun.

So, yeah, amid the tragedies, life in the ER has its lighter moments. Without them, the work would feel a lot harder—and sadder.

PC

AN ADVENTURE
INTO ALCHEMY

Dear Jack,

Psychiatric patients in the ER can be the most difficult patients to deal with. It's a huge issue with the unfunded, or government-funded patients, as it is very difficult for them to get timely care. Their lives are often too disorganized to keep appointments making care even more difficult. So they come to us because we are open 24 hrs per day. Night seems to be a bad time for them and often their acute flare-ups of anxiety or psychosis seem to occur then. And this can result in all sorts of bizarre behaviors.

I was working the all night shift a few days ago. About 4 a.m. I picked up a chart with a chief complaint of "I'm hungry". As I am walking to the room I am starting to feel a bit irritated with this patient before I even meet her. "You are here for a sandwich?" is repeating over and over in my head. WTF? I haven't slept since yesterday and this is how I am spending the last early morning hours of my shift. Even before I get to the room my mood softens a bit as I think this scenario through.

While there is psychiatric care available for unfunded patients the system in Texas is grossly inadequate. An embarrassment really. In a broader view the situation for the homeless seems even more absurd. In our society you can come to the most expensive place for healthcare on a whim. Doesn't matter if your complaint is something that would have been treated with "a bit of Mom's spit" when I was a kid, like a mosquito bite. Today you have access to an ER specialist for these problems. Nowhere else in society is this kind of access for service granted.

Consider the most basic of human needs, food and water. If you are hungry, even starving, you have no right to walk into the nearest grocery store and grab a sandwich and a quart of chocolate milk. You will be thrown out in seconds. Yet you can come to the ER with such a complaint, be seen in a high cost environment, and run up a $1,000 bill society will pay for. And at the same time you can obstruct care for patients more medically in need. And then walk out, quite possibly with a sandwich. Absurdity.

I open the door to the room and my patient is standing at the sink trying to fiddle with the soap dispenser. She is probably about 50 years old, thin, and very unkempt. She has what we call "a street tan". A deep tan that the homeless wear almost as an identity badge. You know at a glance how grim their life situation is.

I say hello and walk over to see what she is actually doing in the sink. Our equipment and supplies are often a target for damage and theft, and I am pretty fed up with going into a room and finding the otoscope or opthal-moscope heads have been stolen again. These are the tools we use to look into your ears and eyes. They have no use for the thief whatsoever as the stolen piece will not work without the rest of the instrument. What I find in progress though is not theft, but absolutely bizarre.

In the bottom of the sink is a Styrofoam cup that she has covered with some paper towel, making a sort of coffee filter shape. And in the center of the makeshift filter is a big wad of chewing tobacco. She is trying to drip hot water from a second cup through this mess for some reason. I ask, "What are you doing Ma'am"? She answers, "I'm trying to make some coffee". What the hell? She is also visibly shaky, suggesting another common problem.

Alcohol abuse is common among the homeless. They often turn to alcohol as a form of self-medication for their anxiety. And, so, alcohol with-drawal is also common. Without a steady income it is hard for them to get their forty-ounce malt liquor for breakfast and by evening the shakes are in progress. I am beginning to feel her pain as she clearly needs help, and am now no longer angry with her presence. I do wonder though what I can actually do to help her.

I patiently explain that a wad of tobacco will not produce coffee. Only a toxic brown liquid. That while this brown liquid may look like coffee it is not even close to being coffee, and it never will be. Also, that the soap she was attempting to add to her little experiment in alchemy will not rectify the situation. But I easily can, and will.

I offer her a cup of coffee. "Two creams and three sugars"? I ask. And over the baseline of her shakes, she nods yes. Before I leave for her coffee I toss her chemistry experiment into the trash. The last thing I need to be doing is treating a potentially fatal nicotine overdose. I recall once having read the book *"Final Exit"* and that drinking a tobacco extract was included as an option. Death after nausea and vomiting, followed by unconsciousness and hours of seizures doesn't seem like a pleasant exit. I briefly consider that maybe she is suicidal. I doubt she has read *Final Exit* though and figure she is simply another psychotic street urchin.

As I walk down to the crash area to get her coffee I am starting to wonder again just what I am going to be able to do for this woman at 4 a.m. in the morning. I doubt she will meet criteria for admission to the psychiatric stabilization unit. I will likely learn she is off of her medications. Receive advice to restart medications she will have no money for, and personally too disorganized to conquer the road to a pharmacy for a refill. And she likely has lost her Medicaid card to boot.

I return to her room and she jumps from her chair and takes the coffee out of my hand in a flash. She reminds me of a hungry bird still in the nest when its mother arrives with a precious worm to eat. I decide I'll get her a second cup. And maybe that sandwich. I have been cautioned about these sandwiches though.

In the ER providing that sandwich is called "feeding the bears". The bears always want food and if they find it somewhere they will keep coming back for more. Although our hearts often go out to these disenfranchised folks we know that providing that sandwich can lead to recurrent visits here. Just for the free sandwich.

I examine her carefully as psychiatric patients can harbor significant problems without even mentioning them to you. What's on their mind is hard to say. Maybe just that acute need for a sandwich. I once had a similar patient presenting with a few minor complaints who had a foul odor about him. He was filthy, likely unbathed for months, and I initially figure that was the source of the smell. Then I noticed that both of his tennis shoes were wet in the area under the laces and toes, and it hasn't rained here in weeks. I remove his shoes and find that part of both forefeet and all of his toes are dead. Wet gangrene and the stench of dead flesh unbearable once exposed to the air. And he wasn't even going to mention it as a problem.

I don't find much on exam of this patient however. Her blood pressure and heart rate are normal, and with full alcohol withdrawal these rapidly become abnormal. So, some minor medical good news. At least this is not full-blown withdrawal syndrome. But what can I really do for her that will make a difference for her?

For reasons I find impossible to fathom the public psychiatric service will not even speak to us until we have performed a series of lab tests and urine toxicology on such patients. It irks me every time. I decide to get this started though as no progress can be made without them. I also decide to get her a sandwich if she will agree to stay for the tests. She of course says yes, and I bring her a turkey and cheese on whole wheat, and I go back to work. I also call our social worker to come and consult. Maybe I can still leave the ER by 7 a.m. when my scheduled shift ends. I could use the sleep.

As expected in this case her labs do not indicate any emergency condition. The urine toxicology reveals some marijuana use, but nothing else. Our ER social worker, each and every one of them a blessing, has already talked with the psych emergency services who surprisingly agree to see her tomorrow. They know her well. She often goes off her medications and ends up like this. Often the wait for those patients who are not unstable can be over a week.

It's now about a 6:45 a.m., and I return to her room. She is curled up in a ball on the gurney, hospital blanket pulled over her head, sleeping soundly. I wake her up and explain what happens next.

She will receive a dose of both of her medications and has an appointment with the psych services at 11 a.m. tomorrow. It's only a few blocks away and she can easily walk there. They will help her get her medications. Most of the time however such patients feel better temporarily after an ER visit and just return to the street. Rejoin their community of homeless psychiatric patients.

Texas has no reasonable way to commit such patients for care. If they are not suicidal, homicidal, or an acute danger to themselves they are free to leave the ER. It is after all legal to be crazy. The system currently in place could not deal with the volume of these patients anyway I think. Between the UT campus and the 15 blocks to Town Lake there are probably a hundred such patients. Camping more or less under overpasses, in the bushes, or in little huts they assemble out of cardboard boxes. It is shameful.

As I am walking down to the helipad where we all park I feel worse and worse about this thin hungry woman and her alchemy experiment. About how little we actually can do for patients such as her. I turn around and go back to the ER. I grab her another turkey and cheese sandwich and two containers of orange juice and head back to her room. She cries to receive this minor gift.

So today I fed the bears, Jack. And probably created more problems down the road than I solved. But for the moment I feel better. Why did I feed her? Because that is all our system had to offer.

PC

YOU PUT WHAT, WHERE?

Dear Jack,

It's Saturday morning, and I am working the early ER shift. Not a lot going on yet, so I should have time to finish up a chart from a previous patient. Just then, our triage nurse walks in and drops a chart on the desk next to me. "You're going to love this one, doc. Shampoo tube is stuck up his ass." We chuckle. As she walks away she adds, "Wait till you hear the story." My interest is piqued as rectal foreign bodies can be a challenge to remove, and I want to hear this story now. The stories are often the most intriguing part of the case. Just why patients feel the need to lie to us about whatever has happened always puzzles me. We are here to help. We really don't care how this happened or what you do with your anus in your spare time. We simply don't. I understand the patient is no doubt embarrassed to be here with this particular problem, but please, give it to me straight. It might help you get better care. I finish up my chart, and pick up his, then walk to his ER bed.

I think about the patients who lie to us. Some are so common, it is almost laughable. The intoxicated patients on Saturday nights with their split lips and facial contusions always are happy to relate exactly what happened. The story is the same. "I was just walking along minding my own business when two dudes jumped out of nowhere and beat me up." Even the details are the same. Someday, I hope to meet these two dudes. Maybe I will kick their asses and send them to the ER to tell their version of the story. These two dudes have caused me so much work over the years, I have grown to dislike them intensely.

I pull back the curtain to bed twelve, and my patient is lying on his side looking rather forlorn. No doubt he's rethinking why his little experiment in proctology has gone so awry. He doesn't appear to be in any distress, though, except for his obvious embarrassment

I ask him the usual questions that are important for his care. How long ago did this happen? Are you in any pain? Have you been bleeding? And, of course, how the heck did this happen? These questions are important. Rectal foreign bodies can turn into a medical disaster if the rectum has been torn, allowing contamination of the pelvic area. Such infections can require surgery, IV antibiotics, and even a temporary colostomy. So, we need to know what we're dealing with here. He finally gets to the "how" question, the part I've been waiting for.

He says he was taking his morning shower and decided to shampoo his hair. "OK," I say, "go on." While he was all soaped up, some of the shampoo got into his eyes and he dropped the shampoo tube to the shower floor. Then, he slipped. It seems the shampoo tube had miraculously landed straight up on the shower floor and stayed that way, waiting to do its dirty work. When he fell, he landed right on the tube. And the tube just happened to work its way right up his ass!

A simple accident. Just an episode of bad luck. Puhlease! I'm not judgmental and I don't care what you like to do in your spare time. Just tell the truth. Oddly enough, I heard this same story years before. Same situation. Same kind of shampoo tube. Prell liquid, both times. And both times such horrible bad luck. I think to myself a more believable story might have been my buddies and I were drinking last night and I got plastered. Passed right out. When I woke up my buddies left a note pinned to my shirt that they had shoved a Prell tube up my ass. See, I could believe that one. Sort of the proctologic version of the "I woke up in the bathtub packed in ice with a note that said, "Go to the hospital. We stole your kidneys."

Well, I tell him, the removal is a bit more complicated. I'll have to do a rectal exam and he'll have to sign a permit in case my attempt at removal results in complications. The rectal exam is easy. Just gloves, lube, and my index finger. Thankfully, I can easily feel the end of the tube and I am thinking great, this may be an easy. I order an X-ray, some medications for pain I will cause during removal, and fill out my portion of the permit. And then I sit and wait. I need to make sure there is no free air visible around his rectum on the X-ray as this would indicate the wall of the rectum has already been torn and will mean a definite trip to the OR. Hospitalization afterwards.

The films return and are normal. I have given him a good dose of pain medication, and he is a bit sleepy. I get an assistant and begin to attempt removal. I can grasp the end of tube with just my fingertips but can't get quite enough traction to remove it. It keeps slipping from my grasp. I ask him to bear down and it moves the tube a little closer, but still a no go. I just can't grip it firmly enough. I go get a pair of ring forceps. These have blunt, rounded ends, and if I am gentle, the odds of injury are slim. I locate the end of the tube and gently slide the forceps up to the tube, grasp it, and out it comes. Nice. No bleeding. I am satisfied. He, on the other hand, is ecstatic. His nightmare ER visit is about to end. Just for fun, as he is all relaxed now and more interactive, I ask if he wants the tube back. "It's still mostly full," I say. He laughs and says, "No fucking way. Just throw it away."

He wants to leave, but I need a follow-up X-ray to check once more for free air. I tell him I will discharge him as soon as the films are back. Plus, I will need to give him a few instructions. And you know me, I can't resist adding, "And be more careful in the shower."

Rectal and vaginal foreign bodies are not all that rare. I have seen vibrators, cucumbers, carrots, rubber, and plastic balls. No gerbils yet though. And once, I dealt with a light bulb. Most of the time I can remove the objects, but sometimes, the patients have to go to the OR and be put under for a safe removal. If I can't feel it with my fingers, it is just too dangerous to remove in the ER.

I'm reminded of a case years ago that resulted in a trip to the OR. The patient's partner lost his grip on a vibrator, and it, of course, got stuck. The day before. I asked him why he waited another day before coming to the ER. "The batteries ran out this morning, doc," he says with a laugh. I do love a patient with a sense of humor, despite the circumstances.

In this guy's case, I go through the usual exam but can't feel the vibrator at all. I order all the necessary pre-op labs and an X-ray. The X-ray returns, showing the vibrator deep in his rectum. There's no way I can remove it. At least the film shows no rectal wall injury. Good enough. I page the surgeon to come down to the ER. Here is where the story gets weirder.

The surgeon comes down, and I throw the films up on the view box to review with him. Yes, he agrees, no apparent injury to the rectum; he will call the OR to get a room ready. But then he pauses. "Pat, what is this?" he asks, pointing to the image of a chicken leg bone on the film that I had overlooked. "Omigod," I say, "That's not in his rectum." No, that chicken leg bone is up his penis in his urethra! I can't imagine how that could have been comfortable inserting. Not at all. I imagine it has served as his homemade substitute for Viagra. The surgeon is nonplussed and simply says he will take that out, too.

About an hour later, my patient returns sleeping on a gurney. The surgeon calls and gives me the rundown and asks if I will discharge the patient for him. I, of course, agree, as I am happy to have had his prompt and willing help. And then things get even weirder.

The patient is awake now and ready for discharge. I hear yelling from his room, but I can't make out what he is saying. He's screaming at my nurse. The nurse comes out and simply tells me the patient is mad and wants to talk to me. Fine. But how can he be mad when we took such good care of him? I go into see him, and he isn't just mad, he is furious.

He threatens to sue me. Why, I ask? Why are you so upset? He screams, "I gave you permission to remove the vibrator, but I did not say you could remove the chicken bone from my dick!" "Do you know how hard that bone was to get in there?!" I can only imagine. But I know this conversation can go nowhere positive, so I simply say goodbye and tell him he is free to leave.

That case was definitely a first.

PC

A 'SIMPLE' CASE OF LOW BLOOD SUGAR

Dear Jack,

   I was working the ER treatment area and got called to come help in the crash area where the lone doc on duty was overwhelmed. I'm always happy for a break out of treatment so I go willingly to see what's up.

   The first chart I'm handed doesn't look like much of a challenge. A seventy-four-year-old woman was found unconscious and brought in by EMS. Paramedics said her blood sugar was dangerously low at thirty-four, but after giving her IV glucose, she is now wide-awake. Your brain really needs a constant supply of glucose to keep working. Any dip in the normal range is dangerous and can result in permanent brain damage. But it seems like the paramedics prevented that, and now it is usually just a routine case.

   I take the chart and head for bed five where she is. She is fully alert and in no distress. For a moment, I am disappointed as I was hoping for something interesting. As I think about this, I realize I wish nothing more for this patient than to be returned to health, happiness, and home. Why do I still sometimes desire something more dramatic from medical care?

   I greet her and her concerned daughter. Sometimes, family members are harder to satisfy than the patient. I get the sense as I shake her hand and look into her eyes she is intelligent and open-minded so my fears of satisfying her pass. This is good, the kind of family member I like.

My patient is a pleasant woman. She takes injected insulin on what's called a sliding scale. This means she measures her blood glucose multiple times per day and adjusts her dose of insulin as needed using a little chart. A different dose every time. This is the best way to manage the problem but requires a patient with the capacity to calculate each time and deliver the right dose. She tells me she has not eaten today and it is now just past lunchtime, so I figure I already know the cause for her low sugar. She knows it, too. She took her usual dose of insulin but simply didn't eat.

The care of the diabetic with any illness always is concerning. What may be a minor infection for others can result in disastrous consequences. Some of them go into what is called ketoacidosis with the most minor upsets in routine, and that is a major emergency. I am happy to hear that unlike most adult-onset diabetics, she has never suffered acidosis. The other issue with elderly diabetics is that sometimes a drop in sugar level is caused by some other illness, most usually an acute infection. Our immune system weakens as we age, and with diabetes, it happens faster. With her history of taking her insulin but not eating, I feel relatively certain that I have the real cause for her sugar drop.

I review her chart and examine her. She has no symptoms whatsoever. Great. Her vital signs are all normal, she has no fever, and even her blood oxygen is in the high-normal range. I congratulate her on not being a smoker and she asks how I knew. I explain that her lungs are still working well, and that tells me a lot. She simply ponders in silence and her daughter smiles and nods.

I'll order a few basic labs and a urine sample to be thorough, but don't expect to find much. Maybe a silent urine infection. I consider a chest X-ray but decide there seems to be no point. She has no cough, no shortness of breath, and no fever. Definitely no need for a chest X-ray. Her daughter asks about a CT scan of her brain to look for a stroke. I sense an argument coming. She does, however, accept my explanation that with no persistent neurological findings and a known history of such a low blood sugar, a CT scan is unnecessary.

I head back down to the treatment area. The daughter's question about a CT scan sticks in my mind and I reconsider. I've done this long enough that I always reconsider patient requests and questions. Sometimes, they are right, something else should be done.

Not very long ago, the practice in Texas was different because of the fear of a malpractice suit. The feared scenario was that you have a patient request testing that does not seem medically indicated, so you follow protocol and refuse to do the test. Then, lo and behold, the patient returns the next day worse. By then it's clear that if you had followed the family request, this wouldn't have happened. If the patient does poorly, or even dies, you have a lawsuit, one you could easily lose before a jury. It's not right, but that fear of a lawsuit drove many doctors to order unnecessary testing. Today, though, we have Texas tort reform, which limits payouts in lawsuits and protects us considerably against this sort of claim. That has eased many a fear, but it hasn't fundamentally changed the way I practice medicine. I am a careful sort by nature and always consider requests for testing carefully. Sometimes, especially with an inexpensive test, I will just order it to satisfy them. But I always explain my thinking. Communication is the key to preventing angry patients and families. It shows you care. Malpractice suits are often about anger, not so much about the actual care. I usually conclude my explanation by saying, "This is what I would do for a family member, and so it is what I will do for you." I sincerely mean it.

An hour or two later, everything I've tested comes back normal. She has eaten a hospital lunch, or at least most of it. Green Jell-O is apparently not one of her favorites so it is left on the tray. But everything else is gone. Her blood sugar has remained normal, and her vital signs haven't changed.

I carefully explain everything to the daughter and patient, but Mom isn't listening much anymore. She feels fine and is ready to leave. Thankfully, however, the daughter does listen. We review my concerns about her mother managing her blood sugar with a sliding scale and the necessity to be careful with calculations. Mom also has to be sure to eat. She shows no hard signs of dementia, but I always worry about this when insulin management seems to go awry. They go home, smelling like a medical rose, and I am satisfied.

Three days later, I run into one of the residents in the hall; he tells me she has been admitted. "Damn," I say. "What is wrong?" I immediately rethink my decision to let her continue to manage her own insulin. He says, "No, no problem with her insulin. She has pneumonia." Pneumonia? Why didn't I get a simple chest X-ray? We could have started treatment, nipped it in the bud. But not doing the X-ray still seems like the correct decision, as she had no signs of fever, cough, etc. Yet she has pneumonia. Did she have it that day I saw her? Maybe it's just now starting up? Or was it the contributing cause for her low blood sugar that I overlooked? I hate such developments in the care of a patient.

I follow her progress over the phone with the resident. I learn she is worsening daily, despite antibiotics. On day five, they decide to get a bronchoscopy to make sure they are treating the right illness.

I fear she will not get better. I feel like I made a mistake, and now the patient is paying the price. I have nightmares about this kind of thing. And following the bronchoscopy, everyone is shocked.

My patient has pneumocystis pneumonia, usually only seen in AIDS patients. What? Pneumocystis? This can't be. But this organism is what is called an opportunistic one. If you are debilitated with a weakened immune system, it can cause disease in patients who don't have AIDS.

Sadly, on day eight, and despite changes in her treatment, I learn she has died. I feel awful thinking about the opportunity I missed to do the chest X-ray. All the doctors say the same thing to me, "I wouldn't have done one, either." Nobody feels like I have erred but me.

I ruminate about my possible role in her death, but I return to a recurring thought: Fate plays a role in our lives. Not predetermination, just the effect of living in a world of statistical probabilities. A rare, unexpected disease can surface and take our life. And there isn't much we can do about. In fact, I don't believe there is anything we can do about it. Even so, I am inconsolable.

We have a saying that comes up frequently at our monthly ER group meetings. "It's a minefield out there." It's a reminder that no matter what we do, eventually, we will step on some mines. I think back to comments my mentor made when I told him I planned to practice emergency medicine. He asked me to reconsider, saying that patients would die under my care, even when I did my very best for them. "Can you live with that?" he asked. "Can you then get up and move on?"

I know I will get up. I will get over this. And, yes, I can go on. But it will take time for my confidence to return. I'll probably get a chest X-ray on every patient for a while. Just because shit happens.

PC

SHE FAINTED.
NOW SHE'S BACK

Dear Jack,

Fainting. Doctors call it syncope. In young people, it's almost always a benign event, though there are exceptions. The big one is fainting while running or exercising, as it can be a harbinger of sudden cardiac death. In older folks, it is a much different matter. Many more medical possibilities have to be considered, and the odds are much higher the fainting signals a significant problem.

I am working the 11 a.m. to 11 p.m. shift; only the all-night graveyard shift is worse. Twelve hours in a busy ER without a rest, eating your lunch and dinner in interrupted gulps is just too much. We are prone to errors the more tired we get. And that's been proven by research. That's why most hospitals have abandoned the once-standard twelve-hour ER shifts. And placed limits on the hours doctors in training may work. Overwork and working while tired are now recognized as the problem they are.

My patient this evening is a delightful seventy-four-year-old woman. The chief complaint section of the chart merely says, "Fainted." As I walk to her room, I am going through the possible causes for her fainting spell in my head. I glance at the chart again and note that her vital signs are all normal. Most likely, this is going to be nothing. Perhaps she just stood up too fast.

Maybe she's a little dehydrated or recently started a new blood pressure medication. I'll just have to see what she says.

Before I go into the room, I call out to one of the nurses that I will need an EKG. It will be a key factor in deciding whether it is safe to discharge her. I figure I might as well get things moving.

As I enter the room, I am greeted with a smile and a pleasant, "Hello, doctor." I like this patient already. A smile goes a long way with me. And I smile back and introduce myself, shake her hand, and sit down next to her. She relates that she just fainted at home, and her friends have made her come to the ER. She has no concerns and simply wants my blessing to leave. I explain in some detail what we need to do and why. I tell her silent heart attacks, blood clots to the lungs, severe anemia, heart failure, and even a problem with her heart's electrical conduction system can be a cause. All of those need to be ruled out. She looks a bit disappointed, having hoped for a quick, "You're fine. Go home." But in a very pleasant voice she says, "Well let's get on with it then." Now I like her even more. A patient who remains pleasant despite her dashed expectations is refreshing. She will allow me to go through the necessary steps before I can turn her loose.

She is quite healthy and active, and my history adds little to her care. She doesn't even take a single prescription medication. No heart history with her or any family members. Just one thing stands out: She does not remember what happened when she fainted. She says she just woke up on the floor and friends told her she passed out. Alarm bells start going off in my head, though not at full volume yet.

Most people who faint remember feeling weak and dizzy as their vision slowly goes black. She remembers nothing. I do a detailed exam looking for common symptoms that might indicate a high-risk patient. An irregular heartbeat, for example. A new heart murmur or a change in a previously diagnosed one. Low blood oxygen. Blood in her stool. Anything to help me decide whether it is safe for her to go home or not. Even her EKG is normal, absolutely normal. She did have a sizeable lump on her forehead, what my

dad called a goose egg. She also mentions a mild headache. She is uncon-
cerned about these as well, but should I be?

I tell her I will go order her lab work. It's not busy so I tell her I should
be back with results in 45 minutes or so. She simply says, "Okey, dokey." As
I walk back to the computer to enter the orders, I reconsider that goose egg
on her head. Usually, a brain CT scan for a fainting episode is a great waste
of resources. Typically, few surprises are discovered. Such scans have actually
made the emergency medicine top ten list of things not to routinely order
with this presentation. I decide to get one anyway given the size of the lump
and her headache. I decide I'm going to be extra thorough with her.

An hour later, all the studies I ordered are completed and I find her
waiting patiently in her room. She's all dressed up, sitting on the side of the
bed, purse beside her, and ready to go home. I explain everything to her.
All the tests are normal. Her exam is normal. I even include an explanation
about the published "syncope rules." These are algorithms developed out of
clinical research that identify patients at high risk for a possible bad outcome
within the next thirty days. She passes those tests too, and I let her know it.
And then I drop the slider in on her. I explain that I don't like the circumstances of her fainting spell, especially the fact that she doesn't remember the
actual incident, had no premonitory symptoms. I tell her my inner voice, my
radar, is beeping and that there could be danger here. I ask her to consider
overnight observation on a cardiac monitor and consultation with the cardiologist in the morning. She politely refuses. It's her right, I know. But I need
for her to understand there is some risk. She says she understands and is not
worried. She will see her doctor next week. I know that in this circumstance I
should get her to sign the "Leaving Against Medical Advice" form to protect
myself, just in case something should happen. But she is such a sweet woman
I just can't confront her with this bit of legalese. I don't want to insult her.
So, we say our goodbyes and off she goes.

I reassure myself her research-developed syncope score indicates
she is low risk. I had even run her through two different risk models on

the computer. I tell myself to quit worrying, and I go back to work on the next patient.

No less than thirty minutes later one of the nurses approaches me. "Your friend who fainted is back," she says. "She is in room nineteen. Fainted again." Damn. I pick up the chart and go right to her. Just as before, I am greeted with a smile and a playful, "I'm back." I simply like this lady. She's got a great attitude. This time, however, she has split her forehead open with the fall and will need stitches. She's sporting a two-and-a-half-inch-long gash. It's deep, too. I tell her, "Looks like you failed the outpatient test. You're going to need to be in the hospital." She answers back very sweetly, "We'll see about that." She is stubborn, but a sweet kind of stubborn at least.

I order a second EKG and another set of cardiac enzymes, along with a suture tray set-up. She wanted me to use glue or just butterfly tapes, but this laceration will need a layered closure. Sutures will need to go under the skin and in the surface of the skin. She is not a candidate for glue or tape.

The nurse brings in my supplies, and we start the procedure. Lidocaine is first injected to numb the area. Then I cleanse and irrigate the wound with saline solution. I cover the area and part of her face with sterile towels leaving one eye uncovered so she can more or less watch what I am doing. I explore the laceration and see her skull directly. No fractures. And then I start the first deep layer of sutures. I have closed so many wounds over the years I am sort of on autopilot. My mind wanders. I keep looking at that eye peeking out from under the surgical drapes as it intrigues me for some reason. And then I realize why. It reminds me of an older neighbor when I was growing up. We had a kind neighbor who used to make me tomato soup and a grilled cheese sandwich for lunch on rare days when Mom had to be away. I can smell the soup and taste that oozy cheese. She always used a lot of butter and I can almost taste that buttered cheese flavor. And this passes my time while suturing.

We're all done, and it is time for the discussion of admission again. She still refuses. I point everything out, including her new laceration. She just chuckles in response, but I finally get her to utter an OK. I make a call to the hospitalist who will admit her and also one to the cardiologist. I want to get a consult from him and I saw him less than an hour ago. He says he will see her tonight before he goes home. Perfect.

About two hours later and much to my chagrin, I receive a call from the cardiologist. He has seen my patient. In fact, he found her slumped over at the nurses' desk upstairs, still in the wheel chair waiting to be moved to her monitored bed. "She was pulseless for 15 seconds!" he says. He says he wheeled her right down to the cardiac cath suite and put in a pacemaker. "Damn lucky for her I was in the hospital and saw her there," he adds. No shit, I think.

He diagnosed her with sick sinus syndrome. It is one of those electrical system problems that occur when the heart's natural pacemaker no longer functions properly. I lamely tell him that she had low risk scores for complications on two different syncope risk tools and that I wanted to admit her the first time. I can almost hear him shrug with disinterest over the phone.

I am relieved my patient will be fine now. I also will always be skeptical of algorithms and computer-calculated risk scores. The score never gives a "no risk" result. It's usually something like, "less than a three percent risk of a bad outcome within thirty days." This is supposed to mean it's safe to go home. But is a three percent risk of sudden death really a fair marker for "safe discharge?" How did this number ever get to be a standard for safety?

You must have complete faith in that inner voice when things don't add up, and listen to it. Never brush off that radar. My mind also drifts to the health worries that occupy the typical person. What we worry about are usually not the things that will cause serious health problems. My patient's attitude of "no worry" was a little too far in left field but more in the ballpark of reality. But I am certain she has not spent the past few years worried about getting an emergency pacemaker on a moment's notice. You just can't really predict the next curve ball life with throw at you.

I also wonder what would have happened if I had convinced her to be admitted the first time and left the call to the cardiologist to the other doctor. Would she have been found in time? Would we have had a good outcome? Would this sweet woman still be alive? Or would she have been found dead in her hospital bed? Fate does seem to play a role in our lives that we can't predict.

Everything ended up lining perfectly for this patient, but will it next time? These are things I worry about. Will all the holes in the Swiss cheese line up and let my patient fall through despite my best efforts? I believe this time, fate intervened and just might have saved her life.

PC

NOTHING REMARKABLE, EXCEPT THE WHEEZING

Dear Jack,

Asthma. Every day we see patients with asthma. Some days, when the weather is changing or the wind is pushing pollen and mold about, we'll see one case after another. And the pollen release of the Mountain Juniper (called cedar around here) can create asthma havoc, just in time for the Christmas holidays. The locals call it cedar fever.

I see asthma as a disease in evolution. Today, it prompts far more ER visits than it did when I was a resident. Sometimes it seems like every kid in Austin has some degree of asthma. Various theories have been proposed to explain this increase, with air pollution high among them. An intriguing theory is that we live "too clean" today, that we need more exposure to allergens, dirt, and dust early in life. That theory is based on the belief that such exposures de-tune our immune system and help reduce the allergic asthma response. I've read peer-reviewed articles demonstrating that infants raised during their first year with a household pet have a significantly reduced chance of asthma.

While in Africa a few years ago, we spent half a day in a Maasai camp. The Maasai people live in large enclosures of thorn bushes piled high, called a boma. These enclosures are used to keep predators out. All of their farm animals, mainly goats and chickens, live inside the enclosure with them. The ground is dusty, and dried animal waste is everywhere, ground into the dirt by the Maasais' bare feet. Their huts are made of mud and straw, the mud gathered from the manure-rich ground in their enclosure. I considered this is a recipe for problems with asthma, so I asked the Maasai "doctor" how he handled severe wheezing and asthma. Over sixty miles of dirt roads separate these people from the nearest hospital or clinic. And with only two Honda 150cc motorcycles for tribal transportation, I imagine this is quite an issue. He replied, "Nobody ever wheezes here. It's not a problem for us." I have to believe there's some validity to the theory that a lack of exposure to allergens early in life may explain the rise in asthma cases.

I was working the 3 p.m. to 1 a.m. shift when the triage nurse brought an eighteen-year-old back to the treatment area by wheelchair. He was wheezing pretty badly. Right away you learn to notice a patients' breathing mechanics. Are they using the muscles of their neck to breathe? Are the areas between their ribs retracting as they try to breathe? Are they also using abdominal muscles to breathe, as well? Can they speak to me in sentences or only gasp out two or three words at a time? These signs give us an idea of how hard they are actually working and how severe the asthma is. Everyone with asthma experiences the sensation of shortness of breath a little differently. Sometimes, minimal wheezing will create a frantic patient and family. Other times, we'll see patients who complain simply feeling short of breath while being able to move only a small amount of air in and out of their lungs. These are the patients who require an extra dose of caution. I can't imagine a severe asthma patient's life, sprinkled with episodes that feel like suffocation and trips to the ER. I know I would not do well with that.

I examine my patient and don't find anything remarkable, except the wheezing. He is working pretty hard to breathe, but I see no reason to be alarmed. I order steroids, a medication that will decrease the inflammation in his lungs and ease his breathing. I also order a nebulizer treatment with a medication that will cause his airways to open up more. He is bad enough that I want him to have a high-dose, hour-long nebulization treatment. It is a more modern way of providing the medication, and I believe, more effective.

I take the chart back to our doctor's area to start writing in it but will keep a close eye on him. He is on the cusp of getting bad but not there yet.

Rarely do we have to paralyze asthma patients, put down a breathing tube, and put them on a ventilator. This is a bad situation and one I hate for the patient and myself. There are simply too many risks for complications. Some complications are fatal if they are not recognized and managed appropriately. One of the biggest dangers is over pressurizing the lungs and causing one to collapse. It's like squeezing a balloon until it pops. If too much pressure builds up in the chest, the heart can't pump blood. It's a cascade of events that can happen in just minutes. At that point, the patient's only hope is an emergency chest tube to release the pressure and re-inflate the lung.

As I am walking back to check on my patient's progress, I recall a patient with a collapsed lung from years past. I had responded to a code blue (cardiac arrest) in ICU during the middle of the night. As I arrived in the room, I could see the patient already on a ventilator and my immediate thought was good, one less thing for me to do while the staff does CPR. I'll have a little time to think. But the ABCs always come first. I listened to his chest and felt for pulses. Good pulses with CPR but I heard nothing but silence from the patient's right lung. I rechecked and compared it to the left, but by now I was sure the right lung had collapsed. While the staff quickly opened the tray with equipment for me to place the chest tube, I stuck a needle into his right chest. And sure enough, air literally whistled out as the pressure was relieved. I knew I didn't have much time, so I quickly gloved up and started the emergency procedure. The needle would only buy me a little time; it's not a cure.

Placing an emergency chest tube in an unconscious patient is generally pretty easy. It takes maybe three minutes, and the tube is doing its job in less than sixty seconds. For this patient, I made my incision, used a hemostat to dissect the tissues of his chest wall toward his head to create a little tunnel, and then, while going through the tunnel and over the top side of a rib, I used the hemostat to pop a hole in his chest. Wow! No wonder this patient had a cardiac arrest. The air and built-up pressure from inside his chest came rushing out in a prolonged whoosh. The tube went in and was placed on suction.

Within a minute or two, the patient's pulses returned, and we stopped CPR. I bandaged up around the chest tube. I called his doctor and let him know what had happened and advised him to come to the ICU. As I walked back to the ER, I felt pretty good about myself. I recognized the problem and quickly treated it. I resuscitated and stabilized the patient. Growing up, I had no idea I would be capable of such things, even though they were exactly what I dreamed of doing. It can be very satisfying sometimes to be an ER doctor, and that was one of those times.

I later learned that my self-congratulatory bliss was premature. Just a day later, the patient died. Brain dead. Too much time had passed between the development of the collapsed lung, progression to a no-pulse situation, staff recognizing the sudden change, and my response time. I was crestfallen. My great save turned out to be the patient's terrible loss. A collapsed lung while on a ventilator requires immediate action, or the patient dies. Every link in the chain of survival has to work in the patient's favor, but sometimes, it just doesn't.

My current patient, however, seems to be doing a bit better. As I examine him, though, I notice he has developed what is called subcutaneous emphysema in his neck. It is air that has escaped his over-pressured lungs from his asthma and has forced its way up into his neck. It feels just like Rice Krispies under his skin. I order another nebulizer treatment and increase his IV hydration. The rehydration is important as it helps liquefy the mucous in his lungs. He needs to cough it up to make his airways just a tiny bit larger.

I am worried about this kid now. This is not a good development. I involuntarily am taken back to other episodes of tension pneumothorax, emergency chest tubes, and ventilators. I don't want to be there again if I can prevent it. I add another drug, a magnesium sulfate infusion and a drip of the same. In some cases, this can help relax the airway muscles and greatly improve the situation. I am hopeful this will work because my patient is reaching maximum medical therapy. I could add what is called non-invasive pulmonary support, a method of helping the patient ventilate his lungs without a breathing tube, but that would increase the pressure in his lungs even more. This would likely make the air leak into his neck even worse. Primum non nocere. I won't do harm by putting him at risk of a complication. Not just yet.

I explain to his mother what has developed. I tell them he is responding to care but not fast enough to suit me. He'll have to be admitted to the hospital. They have been down this road before and are not surprised. But I see them visibly pale when I mention a breathing tube and ventilator. I don't envy their position. I try to console them. He is, after all, getting better.

After two more hours of treatment in the ER, he is markedly improved. He is now talking in full sentences, moving good air, and wants to go home, even though his heart rate is 140 beats per minute. I know this is temporary. A return to normal will take a couple of days. The air that built up in his neck needs to be watched closely as it may increase, though most likely, it will be absorbed by his tissue. His lung may still collapse and require that chest tube. He will go to the intermediate care unit, a step down from the ICU. Big drama in the ER has been averted.

I have learned that avoiding big drama is the best medicine for everyone. Me included. When you are a young ER doc, you seem to live for the dramatic life and death moments. As you mature, you learn that preventing big drama is the real goal. A good friend and longtime co-worker Mike reminded me years ago of the necessity to take satisfaction from routine cases, those without big drama. He put it something like this, "If you depend upon big dramatic cases, cardiac resuscitation, or saving a life for your daily satisfaction, you will be disappointed most days. If you can find satisfaction in the human element of caring for sick people, you will be satisfied every day."

He was right, and today I am satisfied. Good care. Good result. No drama. There is nothing better except the "thank you" I hear from his mom as his gurney rolls up into the hospital.

PC

DOC, I'VE HAD A FEVER
FOR THREE WEEKS

Dear Jack,

My patient and his wife were parked in what we call a "hall bed." Simply a gurney pushed up against the wall as a makeshift care space when we are overcrowded and beyond capacity. It is far from ideal, as you might imagine. The patient has almost zero privacy. And I have nothing--no supplies, no equipment within reach for examining or treating the patient. Few ERs are really set up to handle such patient surges, and today's onslaught is worse than most.

My patient is a sixty-year-old man, who appears worn and haggard. His wife also is weary, distraught, and looking for the answers that have eluded them after visits to three different doctors. He has had a fever now for just over three weeks. My mind briefly flashes back to my own similar bout with prolonged fever and typhus.

I know just how he feels, I'll admit it, I love the mystery fever cases. They're challenging because there are so many possibilities for the cause and so much to sort out. This patient is a refreshing change of pace amid the hordes of flu patients I have seen all day.

We go through the usual detailed history of his illness, past illnesses, known medical conditions, and any recent travel or exposure possibilities.

Nothing notable is mentioned, and no clues surface. It is easy to see how other physicians had probably backed off at this point, suspecting some virus, particularly during influenza season. But the fever that accompanies flu doesn't last for weeks. I am certain something else is going on, something important.

I examine him the best I can in a hallway bed. Often, a careful exam of the skin, the eyes, and the throat area can lead to a clue. Tiny hemorrhages in the surface of these tissues sometimes can offer clues to the patient's hidden infection. But nothing. I look at his nail beds, examine his eyes with an ophthalmoscope, but, again, I uncover nothing of note. His abdomen is also benign. No telltale enlargement of his spleen or liver. Lungs are clear. And then on to the cardiac exam. And despite the noisy ER, the hustle and bustle of staff and patients, I hear it. A very mild heart murmur. I can barely detect a little "whooshing" noise as his heart contracts and moves the blood. A normal heartbeat makes a lub-DUB sound. This might be it. "Have you ever been told you have a heart murmur?" I ask. He answers no. It is so faint I can see how it could have easily been missed during past exams. But it could also be the critical clue I need.

There are still lots of possibilities for this fever, but I am making progress. I am feeling like a real detective. I order a CT scan of his brain to rule out a brain abscess and a CT of his abdomen, which can yield a number of diagnoses explaining prolonged fever. I also order a set of three blood cultures and an assortment of other special lab tests. And then I decide to just finish his work-up completely and order a STAT echocardiogram, a sonogram of the heart. Normally this could wait till he is admitted but I want an answer for them, and me, now. I silently prepare for the argument with the radiologist and, quite possibly, from the cardiologist. They'll likely say the echo should be done tomorrow, or once the patient is discharged and is no longer using ER time and resources. I can already hear them saying, "Why do you need this in the ER on a weekend?" But I am not letting go of this patient until I have an answer. I have been where he is now, and I know it is not a good place. I will exhaust the arsenal of possibilities before I let him and his wife go without a diagnosis.

This echocardiogram will give me a look at his heart valves and might even reveal the cause of the heart murmur. I am thinking he may have something called endocarditis. This is a bacterial infection on the inside of the heart and can occur in various ways. One of the most common causes is IV drug abuse, which is not likely in this man's case.

Bacteria run free in our blood all the time, unleashed many different ways. Even brushing your teeth can send bacteria into your blood. Usually, your immune system easily handles the problem. But, sometimes, the bacteria lodge on the surface of a heart valve and set up housekeeping. There, the bacteria multiple slowly, causing small lumps of material to accumulate called vegetations. If it goes on long enough, this infection can actually destroy the heart valve. Treatment will mean prolonged antibiotics or even a heart valve replacement.

I explain all of this to the family and go back to do my charting while we wait for the echocardiogram and lab test results. The echo confirms that vegetations have formed on the heart valves. I tell the couple that I have an answer for them: He has that heart infection called endocarditis that I had feared. This case can't be handled here, so I talk with an infectious disease specialist and arrange for my patient's transfer. Despite the serious nature of this diagnosis the patient and his wife are relieved to finally have an answer. Again, I know how they feel. They thank me profusely, which lifts some of the dark cloud of grinding through the long shift ahead.

This is what I now call "a good case." I reflect on how my definition of a good case has changed over the years. For young doctors in emergency medicine, a "good case" usually means something dramatic, like a horrible trauma, with lots of blood and broken bones. Or a patient with a collapsed lung requiring a chest tube, or a brain hemorrhage, or some other life-threatening problem. The young ER doc craves these challenges, but they often spell medical disaster for the patient and the family. Calling such cases "good" strikes me as such a hollow definition now.

I long ago left this definition behind. I now define a good case as one that requires deep thought, special care, thoroughness, solving a problem others have missed, and getting the patient on the road to recovery.

As my patient and his wife leave the ER, I notice the waiting room is even more stacked up with flu cases. Time to get back to work.

PC

WHEN THERE'S NOTHING LEFT TO DO

Dear Jack,

I am recalling just after my father died. It was soon be time to spread his ashes and we were all sullen. Alzheimer's disease took him, as you know. We were at Mom's house for his memorial service when someone knocked on the front door. I answered. A man in a dark suit holding a small cardboard box stood by quietly. I signed for the box. It was labeled across the top with Dad's full name in large, bold type. It weighed about four pounds. Inside, the material was very dense, like sand. Just the minerals that remain after cremation. The remains of my own father, now in my hands. As I walked back to the bedroom with the box, I remembered the strong arms that once tossed me in the air, helped me reel in a strong fish, and taught me how to hold a rifle steady while hunting. The Dad who watched my baseball games, who was happy cheering from the sidelines, whether I was playing ball or earning an academic honor. And now, all I had were memories and these four pounds. I put the little box in a drawer next to my Mom's bed. We would spread his ashes together later. And that was that. A surreal and painfully sad moment in my life.

I thought about my father when years later I was called to see a patient in the ER. At the bedside, I see an elderly man who was brought in by his somewhat younger wife and caregiver. Like Dad, he has Alzheimer's. Thin, fragile and a bit hunched over, even while lying on the gurney, I notice the sunken areas around his eyes and the sides of his face. It's what we call "temporal wasting," when the body fat is severely reduced and your face and head begin to narrow. A human being drifting towards death. But his eyes are oddly bright. He looks up rather quickly for someone with late-stage dementia. And he smiles. But upon closer examination, I realize I am mistaken. It is painfully obvious he recognizes nothing, understands nothing, and his smile is simply the result of some deep part of his brain that remains, continuing to act like the normal man he once was.

His wife tells me he has been running a fever for a day and has a cough. No appetite. Not drinking fluids. It is the sadly common presentation of a life moving slowly, inexorably, to an end. A little closer each day.

The exam is unremarkable except for a few crackling noises in his right lung area, typical of pneumonia. His wife and I talk a bit, and I explain what is going on and the plan for his ER care. She seems like a kind and grateful woman. Tired, though, worn from the toil of caring for her dying husband. Lack of sleep contributed to her own sunken eyes and the dark circles below them. Just how my own mother looked after a couple of years of a similar routine. Watching your husband lose his mind and die slowly in front of you is devastating. Medicine has little to offer, and nothing can stop it. Except death.

I go back the chart room and enter the usual orders into the computer knowing what the results will be. His chest X-ray will show pneumonia. His blood count will be mildly elevated, and his sodium a bit low. And that will likely be it. Sir William Osler, considered the father of modern medicine, was the first to call pneumonia "the friend of the aged." It's a relatively painless way to die, slowly slipping off toward that final parting, often while asleep. It has also been called the scourge of the young, and has carried away many an infant as well.

Once I have all of the lab results, I go back to the room to talk with my patient's wife. I explain the situation is what I expected. Pneumonia. Some dehydration. I assure her she has done a great job taking care of him. It is obvious how much she cares. But this may well be his end. Just like so many others like him.

She insists she wants him treated fully. We talk some more. He hasn't recognized her or family members in a year or more. He is spoon-fed and in diapers. He stools without warning, and she bathes him afterwards, sometimes twice daily. All of this is taking its toll on two lives, not just his. After some conversation she relents and agrees to a "no code" status. This means we will not do CPR. We will still admit him to the hospital, start IV antibiotics, perform rehydration and provide other supportive care.

Before he is moved to an inpatient room, I return to speak with her outside. She seems anxious for the conversation. I tell her of my own father and, my mother's struggles at home. I tell her how I watched the same disease take its toll on both of them. She cries as I explain to her I have been there. That as hard as it is, it is time to place him in a nursing home. I tell her that she should not let this disease claim two lives. She has already done everything humanly possible, I tell her. But she is reluctant. After forty years of marriage, she is not ready for this step. I understand, although I hope I have helped her to consider a new path. She is maybe fifteen years younger than her husband and still vibrant. Her husband's life, like my dad's at this stage, is really already over.

A wave of grief washes over me as I watch the gurney and patient roll down the hall, heading to a room in the hospital, with the man's wife at his side. Loyal to the end. Three out of four demented patients at this stage score a zero out of twenty-four points on the cognitive scales commonly used to assess brain function. Yet, their families often request and receive full treatment, despite counseling. The human toll and practical costs of such care are enormous.

A couple of weeks later, the couple is back in the ER. His wife smiles, greets me, and tells me she is glad I am there. She knows I understand. They have the same complaint and get the same lab test and X-ray results. And we talk again. About death, dignity, their relationship, and her deep love for him. I repeat my sadness for him and for her. She has clearly thought about what I said last time and says she is ready to let him go. But not without some treatment. She can't quite let nature takes it course, and I agree.

I arrange a hospice consult. The physician director is a friend of mine. His program has helped ease the passing of many patients and he is an understanding and sympathetic director. One day at lunch, he told me the program had just had its ten thousandth patient.

My patient goes home with his wife on oral antibiotics and pain medications to ease any suffering. I hope it goes as well as it possibly can. I never see the spouse again, but I think about how medicine has failed her. Physicians don't take the time to talk about end-of-life issues with patients and their families, especially earlier in their care when they can make plans during less-turbulent times. I know why they don't. I understand a busy office, the stress and strain of running a practice, and the fact that this service does not pay the bills. I also understand the perception that they have other patients who can benefit from their time and treatment. Who aren't beyond help. But the doctor has a second person who desperately needs help and is being ignored: the spouse.

I wonder about my own future with dementia. Although the usual Alzheimer's is believed to have only a weak hereditary link, my dad's case was of premature onset. This form does have a higher familial link. I remind myself the future belongs to no one. Live your life today. Enjoy each day. No one knows how many you have left.

And then I go back to work.

PC

I'M LEFT WITH COLD SHIVERS AND AWE

Dear Jack,

I was in the doctor charting room, trying to catch up on the cases I had seen that day when a nurse stuck her head in. "Chest pain in room twelve, doc. Eighty-two-year-old man." And with a clack, the chart simply went to the bottom of the rack, below those of a few others waiting to be seen by a doctor. I simply hate this practice. I know that the staff will start the EKG, and even bring it to me for a quick check. They will enter routine cardiac orders, but I don't think medicine should be practiced this way. An eighty-two-year-old patient with chest pain should be seen within minutes. The chart should be at the top of the rack. Medicine is more than tests and EKGs. There is still an art to it. I drop what I am doing and saunter over.

I say saunter because I have been relaxed at work for many years now. Gone is the anxiety that was my companion during residency and the early years of practice. Experience breeds confidence and a sense of calm. I even dress casually. I have worked in hospital scrubs and sandals for so long, I am almost as comfortable here as I am lying on the couch at home, watching a movie.

My patient is lying in bed without apparent distress. He is being hooked up to an EKG machine, and a cardiac monitor is already attached. He is surrounded by a few concerned family members. I start my routine of introductions when, suddenly, I recognize him as someone I know. A kind, dedicated man who is always ready to help. He smiles, and I shake his hand. "What's going on?" I ask.

He says he has been having pain in the center of his chest, with some radiation to his left shoulder and back. He describes it as simply a pressure, like he has to belch, but more severe. Started about thirty minutes ago. This is what we call "typical" chest pain; it's worrisome because it often indicates actual cardiac disease. A wave of tension passes through me, but I try not to show it. I especially like this man and would be aghast if something were to happen to him on my watch. Or any time, for that matter. But he is at an age when bad things tend to happen. I am here to prevent them, if I can.

I glance up at the monitor and see a normal cardiac rhythm of about sixty beats per minute. The nurse hands me his EKG, which I study immediately, expecting the worst. But it appears normal in all respects. A medical history and a thorough exam offer no clues, though I am wary of letting my guard down. I am always suspicious that something unexpected is percolating beneath the surface. That has helped me care for patients many times. This seems, at the moment, though, good news. Nothing obvious is amiss. Acute heart attacks are most often accompanied by EKG changes, and the big one that concerns us most is simply not there. I'm referring to the ST segment elevation, the measurement between intervals on an EKG and a sign of heart muscle starved for blood. Sometimes, very early in a heart attack, the EKG will appear normal. I make a mental note to repeat the EKG in about twenty minutes or so, to make sure no ST elevation occurs. I tell the nurse to leave the EKG monitor leads attached. These sticky little pads will yank the hairs from your chest when removed. I see no reason to put him through that twice.

I explain everything to him and the family members at his bedside. I am concerned, I say, but not alarmed. Could be a lot of things going on. I order an aspirin. Given early, simple aspirin is one of the most effective methods of improving the outcome when the pain is coming from the heart.

It's surprisingly effective and greatly reduces the patient's chance of dying. I also decide to try a little nitroglycerine to see what happens. If this man's pain stems from his heart, it may provide relief and add an important clue. We walk through the routine of sublingual NTG every five minutes for three rounds. Afterwards, he says, "Maybe it's a little better, doc," but not much. I return to the chart room and enter a few more orders. Verbal orders don't work these days, so I must go back to the computer and type them in. That's frustrating when I'm busy, which is most of the time. And now, I will see some other patients while I wait for the lab and X-ray. I will check on him a few times, too. This is not the kind of complaint I am comfortable putting on hospital autopilot, despite the absence of real red flags.

It's a bit later when I hear the automatic cardiac monitor alarm beeping. The alarm and second-to-second heart rhythms are displayed on an array of video screens at the nurses' station. This important center of information is frequently unmanned here, just like in many hospitals. Most of the staff is tied up elsewhere. The clerk is away, too, perhaps restocking supplies. An understaffed ER. Calling this "cardiac monitoring" has bothered me since day one. Jeez.

The display shows my patient's heart rate is down to fifty. In the room, though, nothing has changed. His other vital signs appear normal. His pain is the same as before. His family looks at me for answers. The second EKG I ordered has not been done, and I call for the nurse. I want that EKG badly now, and a few minutes later, it is in my hand. The results: distressingly normal. It's not that I want to find a cardiac problem; I just want answers. Now. Life in the ER just doesn't work that way, though. It isn't like a TV show.

I walk back to my computer, just across the hall, to check for lab results. So far, all I see is the STAT troponin, and it's normal. This test is quite sensitive in identifying dying heart muscle, but if it's done too early, the result can be unreliable. Still, it's better news than an abnormal result. Checking the monitor, I see his chest X-ray has been completed but not yet read. So, I pull it up on the computer for a look. Crap, I shout silently. The shadow of his

185

mediastinum, an area in the center of his chest, is abnormally wide. Clearly, too wide. I don't need a radiologist to tell me this could be an aortic aneurysm. This type of aneurysm is an abnormal dilation of the aorta itself, often the result of years of high blood pressure, smoking, or too much cholesterol. The aorta can simply tear apart and rupture, causing immediate death. Or the lining of the aorta can tear loose from the aortic wall and kill a person. His pain may be the result of one of these catastrophes. Now, my radar is blaring louder than the heart monitor. This is a true, life-threatening emergency.

After quickly explaining my concerns to the already worried family, I explain I will order an emergency CT arteriogram of his chest. That test will show whether it's an aneurysm or the condition called a dissection in which the lining of the aorta tears apart. As is sometimes the case with the elderly, the family is much more upset than the patient. He simply offers something like, "Do what you need to, doc." He seems willing to accept whatever is in store for him. It fits his personality exactly. This kind, elderly man has great faith and is ready, whether the outcome is life or death.

I have the clerk call radiology to tell them I want this study right now. No waiting. No excuses. And just like I want, he is rolled off to the scanner. I caution the tech to watch his monitor closely. The dropping heart rate concerns me.

A few minutes later, an overhead page calls for a doctor to come to radiology. Something bad has happened. The scanner is just across the hall, and I am there in seconds. His heart rate is now in the upper thirties, dangerously low. Other vital signs remain normal. Chest pain, the same. The nurse now stays in the room with him as I return to the ER. I want the radiologist on the phone, as I need immediate answers. But it's the weekend. Nothing happens the way I think it should on the weekend. Short staff throughout the hospital. One radiologist is likely reading studies for the entire hospital, from home. It's just one more thing I hate about medical practice and bean-counting hospital administrators. They don't seem to understand that emergencies do not respect weekend hours or weekend staffing. If anything, our volume is a bit higher on the weekends. Every weekend I work, I still ask myself how it makes sense to have a skeleton crew on hand.

Fortunately, today's CT scanners are very fast and provide terrific images. My patient is back in the ER bed within a few minutes. I pull up the CT scan and scroll through it. Yes, an aneurysm. No bleeding around it and no sign of a dissection. That's when the lining of the aorta is being stripped away. This likely means this aneurysm is chronic and not the cause of todays problem. What the hell is going on? I desperately need to know.

Back at the bedside, only a single family member has remained. The others left for coffee, probably thinking the scan would take longer. The nurse is still with the patient, and while I am explaining the scan, his heart rate drops to the upper twenties and his eyes roll back. Shit! I order a STAT dose of atropine IV. This medication is available in seconds, as the code-blue cart has been rolled into the room. I am thankful there are still a few medicines I can get my hands on in seconds without a nurse having to leave the room and get what I need from the big machine that stores everything. It won't unlock or yield the medicine until someone enters billing data on the patient.

His blood pressure is now a little low, but he is still breathing adequately. I order another dose and ask for the cardiac pacemaker leads to be placed. His daughter is at his head whispering to him, "Come on, Daddy." She is convinced he is dying right before her eyes, and I think she might be right. It takes a couple of minutes to get the pacer pads and machine hooked up. Then, his blood pressure drops lower. I order yet another round of atropine, hoping maybe this dose will buy me some time. But it doesn't. His monitor is flatlining.

At this point, the medical response is cut-and-dried. It's all laid out in algorithms in the Advanced Cardiovascular Life Support manual that we ER docs know so well. I am often asked if I don't start to freak out when things get to this point. I always answer no. A monkey could run the code, as it is all predetermined. The real key, I explain, is preventing the case from getting to this point. I have failed in that regard.

We start cardiac compressions briefly and call out for help. The compressions are interfering with getting the external pacemaker fully attached to his chest, so I order them to stop for a few seconds. The pacer is all that can save him. One nurse is pulling out epinephrine, and someone else is preparing him for intubation. Someone asks if he is dying, and in a moment of overly confident theatrics, I say, "Nobody is going to die on my shift today." Quite possibly, that's a lie. While his daughter is saying, "Come on, Daddy, don't leave us," I move up to his head and shake his shoulder and say something like, "Come on. Help us. Come back. You have more work to do." With the pacer in place, I turn it on at a high output to insure rapid capture of his heart rhythm and the correct pacing. And it works. His heart rate goes up to seventy-two. Blood pressure is normal. I imagine my sigh of relief is audible down the hall.

Within moments, he is awake. I slowly dial down the external pacemaker output. It causes chest muscles to contract painfully at high outputs. I want him to be more comfortable, but I also want the pacer to provide a high enough output that it still captures and creates a heart rhythm. His daughter offers thanks and I start making calls for a transfer to a cardiac specialty center.

The CT scan was confirmed to show some aneurysmal dilatation but no dissection and no rupture. It's pure cardiac disease, called sick sinus syndrome. It's more common in the elderly and causes the heart's own pacemaker to simply quit. If it had happened at home, he would be dead now.

All that is left for me to do is send him to a cardiac specialty hospital by helicopter as fast as we can. And, almost miraculously, the helicopter is already on the pad. Off he goes.

A few weeks later, I am working a shift and I see my patient, standing at the desk, waving me over. "Hi, doc," he says. "I wanted to come by and say thank you." I tell him I am glad to see he's doing well. I then explain I am really busy but happy he came by. In ER medicine, rarely does a patient you may have actually saved return to thank you. It is very gratifying. I want to linger and hear the rest of what he has to say, but I have no time at the moment. Two potentially bad patients are waiting on me. He says he will wait, as he really wants to talk.

About twenty minutes later, he is still there, waiting patiently. He says he wants to tell me what happened. I can pretty much guess what he will have to say: He took a helicopter ride, he had some more tests done, they put in a permanent pacemaker, and he is doing well. Maybe impressive for the patient, but to me, a bread-and-butter scenario. But no, that's not what he wants to tell me at all.

He says that during his cardiac arrest, he left his body. He was floating above the room looking down, watching what was happening. He felt calm and at peace watching the drama unravel. Simply watching from above. No worries. Just peace. And he heard the things we were saying, heard the requests from his daughter and me not to leave, to come back. Heard me say he still had work to do. He then drifted back down to his body and suddenly he was awake, lying on the gurney with everyone around him. The pacer connected to his chest was keeping him alive.

His account leaves me with cold shivers and awe. And, of course, lots of questions. Like, what really happened? Was he hallucinating? Or was that his soul leaving his body? The accounts of patients who have had near-death experiences are strikingly similar. Often a sense of rushing upward, bright lights, and the feeling of complete and utter peace.

Just what does it mean? I wonder, as the man who was unconscious recounts everything that was said. Is this what's in store for each of us at that final moment? Fascinating. But I'm in no hurry to find out for myself. After a few moments of pondering it's back to work. Patients are waiting. Always there are more patients.

PC

HUNTING A ZEBRA

Dear Jack,

I was totally consumed in medical sleuthing yesterday, or perhaps, I was engaging in self-actualization, as the psychologists call it. That's the contemporaneous realization and fulfillment of one's talents and potentialities. I was totally immersed in trying to unravel a medical mystery and loved every second!

I was called back to the crash area to see a prisoner who was brought in with a history of vomiting and diarrhea. Pretty routine stuff. I am wondering just why and how these complaints bought him a ticket into the expensive crash area. I was in no rush. I put a few orders into the computer and figured I could get some charting done while I waited for the labs. Nothing sounded pressing at all. But that little voice in my head and my own sense of curiosity got the better of me. Within minutes, I was hustling down the hall to see my patient.

The truth is, I should have done that first. I hate leaving patients triaged to crash and just entering orders for care without seeing them. We call this practice "dry-labbing." In college, that's when you write up the experiment without ever completing it. I wondered on my trip down the hall just why this patient was triaged to crash. I am already thinking I may move him to the treatment area, the place where we handle less-critical patients.

I find him handcuffed to the gurney. A police officer is standing on the right side of the patient, who is in no apparent distress. In reality, we rarely have problems with patients transferred from jail, but, just in case, a police presence is welcome.

My mind flashes back a few years to an incident in which a cuffed patient escaped the ER. She was a young woman with pelvic pain. The officer had cuffed her leg to the stirrup of the exam bed and left the room. Little did he realize that the stirrups were removable. As soon as he walked out, she slid the stirrup off of the table, and clad only in an open-back hospital gown, headed out the door at full speed with the stirrup still cuffed to her leg. My great friend Travis tossed his stethoscope on the bed and started off in hot pursuit. I expected a quick capture; Travis is a supreme runner. I have run with him many times and it is taxing. I tell myself she is as good as caught. He is gone for maybe ten minutes and returns empty-handed. "That chick is a real runner," he says. "Once we got to I-35 I quit chasing her. The last I saw of her was her bare butt headed east." We share a brief laugh. I imagine she is now somewhere in East Austin, still running with the metal stirrup jangling noisily. If the police really want her back, perhaps they should look for her on the University of Texas' women's track team.

I glance at the heart monitor as I approach my patient's bed. The blood pressure cuff has not yet been attached but the heart rate is 120 beats per minute. High, but not alarming. A heart rate of 120 alone won't get you a ticket to crash, so, my interest is piqued. The nurses usually make good calls when they triage patients, and it's up to me to decide if he's in the right area.

As often is the case, prisoners can be difficult. Coming from jail rather than the street, the usual problem is simply being uncommunicative and not outwardly interested in their care. Patients who come in from the street are sometimes assaultive and dangerous. Recently, one nurse had the end of her finger bitten off.

My patient's chief complaint says, "vomiting and diarrhea." Nothing else. When I question him directly, he simply says, "I have diarrhea, doc." He denies vomiting. Maybe he has a little nausea, he says. Must be some case of diarrhea, I think, for a twenty-five-year-old man to have a heart rate of 120. He must be pretty dehydrated. He offers little else and simply ignores further questioning. Like most patients, he fails to realize I am not a magician. Patients tell us what is wrong with them, and then wait for us to fix them. Given a patient with the power of speech that I can't examine versus one with no speech but open to an exam, I will take the power of speech every time.

My exam reveals nothing, really. Just his elevated heart rate. I put a blood pressure cuff on and it measures eighty over sixty! Dangerously low and completely unexpected. I ask further questions, suspecting maybe a gastrointestinal bleed. Have you had any black stool? Did you see any blood? Has this ever happened before? He answers a simple no to everything. Looks like it is going be a routine case of bad diarrhea and some dehydration, I surmise. Not interesting at all.

He has been in prison for a few months so a drug overdose is unlikely. But I can't completely rule that out because I've learned that prisoners and their guards frequently conspire to get drugs. Still, this always amazes me for some reason. Just how could that happen in prison? Despite my years of practice, perhaps I am still a bit naïve.

I put in a few additional orders and increase the normal saline infusion I've ordered up to two liters. I call the nurse over and point out the unexpected urgency to the case. EMS has already left, so there is no further history available to me. I mosey back to the treatment area to await labs and catch up on my charting. Always, there is charting to do.

Perhaps twenty minutes later, I return to the bedside to see where we are with the case. His blood pressure has come up to ninety over sixty. Still low. I attempt to get a little more information from my recalcitrant patient before I am satisfied with that it's just a bad case of diarrhea. I get more of his cold shoulder but finally extract, "I just crapped once, doc." Wait, just one loose stool? Alarms are starting to go off in my head. Something else must be going on.

Hypotension, or low blood pressure, in a previously healthy young person almost always means a reduced circulating amount of blood volume. Usually, simple dehydration or maybe something far more serious: a gastrointestinal hemorrhage. Neither seems to be the case here. A number of other, more esoteric, diagnoses flash through my mind. I wonder, am I just looking for zebras when I am simply staring at an ordinary horse? Hunting zebras is what we call it when the doctor is searching for some exotic disease when the patient really has something common. The adage is, when you hear hoof beats, look for horses, not zebras.

But I don't hear hoof beats. I realize a heart attack can rarely occur at this young age, but I order an EKG to see what it might reveal. Heart failure can be brought on by a viral infection. I order a STAT chest X-ray to have a look at his heart and lungs. It could help. A rare presentation of adrenal failure is also possible, but the labs I have already ordered will screen for this.

It occurs to me this guy is probably just lying. Probably crapping his pants hourly for the past twelve hours and just embarrassed to say so. I order an unusual third liter of saline as I have nothing else to offer except supportive care. And supportive care has saved many a patient while their doctor tries to solve the mystery.

The EKG returns, showing no evidence of a heart attack. Just the rapid heart rate. The portable chest X-ray also returns and similarly offers little help. I notice the heart silhouette on the X-ray looks a little odd and head over to radiology. A radiologist looks and says, "Nah, there is nothing there I would call abnormal, Pat." So, maybe I am chasing zebras after all. I slowly return to the crash area to ponder further.

That heart silhouette continues to bother me, though. And I'm not quite sure why, except I do have a sick patient to care for and the radiologist doesn't. Sometimes when your only tie to the case is an X-ray, it is too easy to rule things out. I show the film to a couple of partners who are working with me and I get the same response. "Normal, dude." Or, "Look for something else."

Jeez. Now, I am sleuthing. Reconsidering everything I know about this patient and his presentation. As well as the limited lab results now available, which are not helpful. I restudy the X-ray, pretending I have never seen it. Take a fresh look. Scouring every anatomic landmark for a clue. And then I see it!

There is just a sliver of metallic density in the heart's shadow, hidden on the X-ray because it is overlying a spinal vertebra. What the hell is that? I order a portable lateral chest view. That may help. The usual view is from the front, and a side view might show something very different. Imagine a picture of a piece of pipe that is directly facing you versus a side view of that same pipe. You see something totally different. I recall the radiologist adage, "One view is no view."

The lateral view returns, and I throw it up on the view box. HOLY CRAP!!! Now the metallic density, as small as it looked, is actually five or six millimeters long. What is it? Prior trauma? Prior surgery? I saw no postoperative scar. And then like a ton of bricks it hits me, that metal density is the broken end of a syringe needle!

More questions for the patient. Do you use IV drugs? When was the last time? Have you ever lost a needle when injecting? To my surprise, and satisfaction, he says he has lost needles twice. I think he is getting the picture that he may be in deep shit and has decided to be more cooperative. Both lost needles were in his groin, a place IV drug users inject when their veins are too damaged, or they are trying to hide their abuse. One needle, he says, he removed using a razor blade. Came off just under the skin. The other needle he never found and figured it was just lost somewhere, probably on the floor.

I now suspect I know exactly what is wrong. That broken off needle in his groin from months ago has sailed up his femoral vein and now has docked in his heart. In fact, the needle has pierced his heart, causing bleeding into the sack that surrounds it. The pressure from the blood trapped in the sac eventually compresses the heart and impairs its ability to refill with blood. We call this pericardial tamponade, a life-threatening condition. Fortunately, my attention to supportive care and the ABCs of emergency medicine have resulted in the exactly appropriate initial treatment. IV fluid replacement to raise the pressure in the right side of the heart and improve cardiac filling. X-rays to probe further. Following the ABCs has never led me astray.

I call radiology for a STAT chest CT scan. No, we aren't waiting for lab work. I want it NOW. "This is an emergency," I tell the radiology tech. And, in minutes, he is in the CT area with me, watching the scanner screen. The images start popping up. And, lo and behold, they confirm there is blood leaking around his heart and obstructing blood flow through it. You can actually see the needle sticking out a couple of millimeters from his heart. Damn, what a find!

I call the cardiovascular surgeon who has the patient moved to the operating room immediately. Fortunately, he was in the hospital and free to start a case. And off the recalcitrant prisoner goes to have his life saved. A long-forgotten needle almost taking his life.

I learn later he did well. When the surgeon opened the sack around his heart to drain the accumulated blood, the needle was immediately visible sticking through the wall of his heart. He simply grasped it with a hemostat and pulled it out. The tiny hole it left behind bled only minimally and needed no further care, so, he simply closed him up.

This case is so bizarre I remain dumbfounded through the rest of my shift. Elated that I got to the right diagnosis, of course. But it is busy in treatment and I have work to do. No time to share this case with my friends, despite being anxious to do so. And I work until my shift ends at 11 p.m. Now I can't call friends to discuss this freaking case because they will all be asleep. There will be nobody to talk to about it tonight.

But I do get to drive home in the cool, quiet night. As I go over what happened, I thank my lucky stars and am simply elated with the outcome. Now I know exactly why his blood pressure wouldn't come up. A needle through the heart. Damn! Who'd have thunk it?

PC

PRIMUM NON NOCERE

Dear Jack,

Primum non nocere. This phrase is among the first Latin words we heard in medical school. I say heard, not learned, because I don't think any of us really "learned" them. Certainly, nobody really understood them. The English translation is, "First, do no harm." This simple dictum can take years to fully comprehend. Some physicians never seem to get its far-reaching implications or embrace it.

I'm in the ER today, and, as usual, I am quietly frustrated and somewhat disappointed in what I see in medical practice. What's under my collar today is the practice of over-prescribing. The right pill can solve anything. Oh, you aren't sleeping well? We have a pill for that. Both patient and physician are complicit here, and both contribute to the problem. Physicians want to help, patients want help, pills await. With a few scribbles on the prescription pad, the die is cast. The patient leaves satisfied. Isn't this how it's supposed to work? Today, everyone is happy. That temporary happiness, though, is often contrary to our guide, *primum non nocere.*

I am seeing one of my first patients of the morning. An older woman is brought in by family members who say she just isn't "all there" again this morning. This is an all-too-common complaint that typically ends in the ER without a clear answer. The patient's workup can be vast, time-consuming, and expensive. The cost of medical resources chasing down such complaints is staggering. Maybe today's case will end differently. Who knows?

When time allows, I like to review the patient's medical records for a few minutes. It can help tremendously as most of our patients are complete strangers. A surprising number neither know their own medical history nor the names and doses of their medications. We don't always have time to check any of this when the ER is busy. This patient's vital signs are fine. The problem sounds more chronic than acute. I have the time to do some checking, so I take the opportunity.

As much as some of my colleagues complain about this, the electronic medical record is my friend, even in its current infantile state. All of the inpatient hospital records are here. At the touch of few buttons, I see admission summaries, consultant's notes, complete care records, lab results, and imaging reports. At one time, this required an hour or two to retrieve paper records from storage. And then time to leaf through maybe hundreds of pages. You can see why this step was frequently omitted. Today, I have little excuse for not knowing more about my patient.

But it's no panacea. The major failing of the electronic record continues to be little, if any, integration with records from outside the hospital. I can see what happened in the ER a week ago, a year ago, or longer, but I can't see what has happened in their doctor's office. I can't see what the practitioner who knows my patient best wrote about her. As U.S. medical care has evolved, we become more dependent on specialists and specialty consultation. Patient care becomes fragmented. Lines of communication fail. Often nobody really understands the patient's complete picture.

As I peruse her record, I am shocked by the number of medications she takes each day. The chart lists fifteen or so meds. She takes the usual stuff: blood pressure medications, oral diabetes medications, stomach acid controllers. Some days it seems like everyone over sixty is taking these drugs. I note that she also takes the more problematic psychoactive medications, the ones that change the way our brains work. They readjust various chemical transmitters in the brain to try and improve the patient's symptoms. Depressed? Maybe you need more norepinephrine to balance things out. Let's try that. Can't seem to get to sleep? Maybe you just need melatonin, or perhaps a benzodiazepine or even a tricyclic antidepressant. Or you just might simply try over-the-counter Benadryl (diphenhydramine). Oh, you can't stay asleep? I see. You need a long-acting sedative. OK, you get the picture. We play roulette with the patient's brain chemistry. *Primum non nocere?* Not really. And a lot of chances to cause problems.

As I walk to the patient's room, I ponder the symptoms and the medication list. As I said, I am frustrated and disappointed. This does not even seem like an ER case; she should be in the office of the physician who knows her best. My job is to make sure nothing acute is going on. I need to decide whether it's something that needs attention now. Maybe a stroke, maybe sepsis, maybe low blood sugar, perhaps, a UTI. The list of possible diagnoses for this confused, elderly woman is quite long. Other problems can be handled by her own doctor in the office later.

As I enter the room I take the gestalt of my patient and the family members who are present. I see a sweet grandma in no distress. She smiles. Worried looks are worn on three other faces. I introduce myself to each of them. We shake hands. This important step establishes communication and is simply polite. It also gives me more information. Touching is important. It establishes care and concern. Their understanding that I do care will improve communication and lead to better answers. It boosts the chances they will ultimately take my advice. It is worth the time, although many ER physicians simply skip this step. Skip the touch, and everyone suffers.

I perform a thorough history and physical exam, all the time conversing with the patient. It may seem like I am making simple conversation, but I am gathering data. I see how she responds. What she remembers. How she is actually thinking. For the practice of medicine, given the choice between being blind, deaf, or mute, I will always take blind. Listening is often more often important than seeing.

Her problem seems chronic, having developed over a year or more. On some days, she is worse; other days are pretty normal. Family members are worried about Alzheimer's, strokes, or some other neurological condition. I try to reassure them based on what I have seen so far I don't think they are the problem. Everyone wants CT scans, our magic looking glass into their insides. Lots of lab work, too. The solution to everything seems to be tests — and more tests. Today's problem is far simpler, I believe, but I have to sell them on it.

I'm focusing on a simple side comment from a care provider. "Oh, you can't sleep? You might try over-the-counter Benadryl, or some similar sleep aid." And that is exactly what has happened. Benadryl. She takes two most every night before bed. The patient assures me it has worked wonderfully. She falls asleep quickly and stays asleep. As I begin my explanation that it's part of her problem, I immediately encounter the usual defensive posture. Who is this ER doctor who offers a criticism of my family doctor I know and love? The one who has helped me so many times? He or she told me to do this, and I am sleeping better. What does this new guy think he knows that my doctor doesn't?

Benadryl at bedtime puts many to sleep admirably. But it is slowly metabolized and can, and will, cloud the next day's thinking. That's especially true in the elderly. And it slowly will build up to a low chronic presence in their system. Worse yet, are its anticholinergic effects, the kind that inhibit certain nerve impulses. Benadryl in the elderly can turn a normal brain into a cognitive mess. I explain all this. I offer some basic lab tests and a few hours of observation.

Predictably, all the lab results are normal. It's now early afternoon and the family agrees, now she seems fine. I ask her to do two things. One, stop the Benadryl. Experiment with other known therapies, like cognitive and behavioral things. No caffeine. Go to bed when tired. No late afternoon naps. My second recommendation addresses her hallowed medication list, even though she and her family are convinced all fifteen are essential. Sit down with your doctor, I tell her. Explain your concerns about so many medications. Ask if you still really need all of them? Remove those with psychoactive properties, if possible. If your doctor won't participate in this, find one who will.

The older brain is particularly sensitive to the side effects of these medications. The unintended consequences of our attempts to help with symptoms can have far-reaching consequences. More medicine is our default response to many problems, even when the answer often is simple. Relax in the evening. Read a book before bedtime. You will sleep better.

Have back pain? Is the answer ibuprofen, hydrocodone, muscle relaxants, and more pills? No. Try some yoga I say. Lose some weight. Strengthen your core. The back pain will likely get better. Not as easy as taking a pill but ultimately more effective. And less dangerous. The patient must participate in their care. *Primum non nocere*. How easy to forget in the daily hustle of practice. How often not fully understood.

"To cure sometimes, to relieve often, and to comfort always." These words, believed to be a fifteenth century folk saying, endure as beautiful poetry and a guiding light for all of us in medicine.

PC

P.S. About ten days later, I am greatly surprised to find a thank you card in my workplace mailbox. Mom is really doing well, it says. I am gratified.

A DEATH IN SLOW MOTION

Dear Jack,

Today, a patient sent me back in time. Back to a time in my career that was especially dark with death. It was that look on his face that triggered it, those unmistakable ways someone's face changes with severe chronic illness. I think of it as a death in slow motion.

Not knowing what to expect, I pick up the next chart from the rack and start down the hall to his room. A quick glance at the box labeled "chief complaint" yields only "shortness of breath." That's a relatively vague medical complaint with many possible causes. The chief complaint is what the triage nurse distills from a summary of symptoms that led the person to come to the ER. Typically, it's your major symptom. It frequently becomes your label during the stay. How's that guy down in fifteen, you know, the one with shortness of breath? We rarely use their name. Depersonalization is a primary survival mechanism in the ER.

My patient was in one of the private rooms down a hall I've walked so many times, with the door closed. I opened it and stepped in, and knew in a second what was wrong. Two young men, probably in their mid-thirties, looked up hopefully. The patient was horribly obvious, lying on the gurney, a sheet pulled up around his neck. It was his gaunt, almost skeletal face, sunken eyes, and brief attempt at a smile that revealed too many teeth, with lips drawn too far back, that caused me to time travel. It's that sneer of approaching death, I think.

To the uninitiated, this look is a bit frightening. I don't fear death. Well, maybe the process of death. But I consider my eventual end to be part of the natural course of things. What frightens me is how I got old enough to consider that the possibility of death is now a real one. Where did all of that time go?

The two men are a couple of decades younger than me and are looking at me for help. I introduce myself and shake their hands without wearing my latex gloves. At this moment, I know very well, the touch of a fellow human being seems extremely important. It starts to establish the rapport and trust, without which, I would be crippled in my efforts to care for him. A patient who trusts you will yield a much better history and is much more likely to follow your counsel. I am not afraid of catching his disease and want him to know it. Right after primum non nocere, "First, do no harm," stands the second dictum: "Comfort always." He seems a bit surprised and relieved, which saddens me unreasonably. Likely, he's been shunned by others because of his frightening skeletal appearance. People fear catching his disease. I hope these two are thinking they may have found a friend. Because they have.

I briefly slip into a reverie, back to a devastating time in the latter half of the 1980s. Too many of those days yielded another dying young man. They usually arrived early in the morning, at the very start of my shift. Each day serving up your first hideous task. I came up with a possible explanation for these routine early appearances. I imagined a conversation the night before between partners, or maybe the patient and a friend. "It's time to go to the hospital. You need help. Tomorrow morning we go. OK? Promise me you will go." And shortly after the morning sun rises, they come, keeping their promise to each other.

Without a doubt, it took a special courage to come to the ER in those years. Ostracized by society, these patients must have felt very alone. Going to the hospital to face the doctor in a last-ditch cry for help when many of them already knew there may be little, or none, offered. At the same time, death was just outside the door in a very real and final way. Yes, a very special courage, indeed.

Many of us at that time considered these patients an unnecessary burden. It was their lifestyle that caused this problem, and now we had to deal with the messiness of their illness and their final days. Many medical providers believed they would catch the disease while providing care. Some actually did. The seemingly trivial error of an accidental needle stick, a splash of blood into the eye, or an open scrape coming into contact with the patient's bodily fluids. And, then, boom, another life claimed. One of our anesthesiologists became HIV-positive after a needle stick and died of AIDS. That made the care of HIV patients seem very dangerous.

Early on in the AIDS crisis, I began to think of them as the walking dead. The medical equivalent of a zombie. We had little help or hope to offer them. We could maybe prolong their life a little bit, but death was coming as surely as it had come to many of their friends. I feel like I should apologize for the way this sounds and explain further.

You understand the necessity of using distance as a shield to somehow protect yourself. And along with the gallows humor that's so common in the ER, depersonalization seemed our only defense against so much relentless grief. It was much more comfortable to regard them as a nuisance and not as a fellow human being. And so wrong for the patients.

Decades later, we are more enlightened. I start with my patient's history and physical. He relates that several months ago, he had lost his insurance benefits and had quit taking his HIV medications. I ask if he had tried to qualify for Medicaid and he said he had but was refused. It is likely at that time he had some savings, probably a car, maybe a house. Regardless, it was too much income that calendar year, and he couldn't qualify for Medicaid until he had lost almost everything. That's how it often goes with public programs. I imagine he was told, "We can't help you now, but come back when you are penniless. Then we will see."

I ask about his viral load and his CD4 count. For years, virtually every HIV patient now knows these critical numbers. The viral load is simply an estimate of how many viral particles are circulating in the blood. The CD4 count refers to a special type of white blood cell that tells me how crippled a person's immune system is. My patient may know other numbers that indicate more about the stage of the disease and his response to prior treatment. These numbers can tell me right away how bad his condition is and which diseases are most likely. Both of his numbers are bad. Really bad, and I suspect I know which opportunistic infection he has even without an exam.

It is called pneumocystis carinii. A weird little protozoan that sets up housekeeping in your lungs when your immune system is crippled. It slowly destroys your ability to exchange oxygen and breathe normally. There are treatments that will help, but we also must re-establish his immune system or all of the treatment in the world will be of no use.

I start my formal exam, and for this, I don gloves first. I know he won't mind now. Rapport has been established. The only really notable finding is the white plaques in his mouth. This is thrush, just like a baby might have, but in his case, a confirmation his immune system is not working well. The only other thing is, of course, his shortness of breath. I get him up off the gurney just to walk a bit inside the room and it is clear that even this activity is a major burden.

I return to the chart room a bit sullen. Our medical system for those without insurance of some sort is almost as sick as my patient. And it has failed him. Today, the vast majority of HIV patients on a full anti-viral cocktail appear pretty healthy. They feel good. These medications work so well I rarely see full-blown AIDS cases anymore except when the medications have been stopped for some reason. Usually, it's financial. I order the labs and X-rays and wait. I return briefly to their room and offer a cup of coffee. It's all I can do right now. He declines; his partner accepts.

Many experts report a recent increase in HIV cases. There are many reasons. New strains of drug-resistant HIV are popping up in communities.

Manufacturing limitations of first-line antiretroviral drugs loom. The IV drug abuse epidemic also contributes. And a lack of sufficient funding applied to the global HIV/AIDS problem continues. Unfortunately, and ironically, partly because the drugs work so well right now, many young gay men have lost their fear of HIV. Another tragedy in progress, I think.

The chest X-ray returns and seems to confirm my fears. I see the characteristic butterfly-shaped infiltrates in the center of his chest. In this setting, it's almost certainly pneumocystis. There's no need for a wild hunt through loads of lab work to find your diagnosis, or at least there shouldn't be.

I really need nothing else at this point and return to my patient's room. Likely, I'll be confirming his own suspicions. He will need hospital admission, an infectious disease consult, a pulmonary consult, and a bronchoscopy to take a sample from inside his lungs. I hope he also gets an experienced, caring internist and the all-important social worker visit to help find him some funding and acquire the medications he will need. He will also need referral to one of the clinics that specialize in keeping HIV patients healthy. Of all of the needs on this list, all we can provide here is the social worker. There are no special clinics or programs for him in our community. He will need to be transferred.

They want to drive themselves to the next hospital. I understand they drove themselves here but am concerned he will go home instead. Return into hiding with his illness. I've seen it too many times and want to make sure he gets the help he needs. His oxygen saturation is tolerable as it is but a bit low, so I add some low-flow oxygen by nasal cannula to justify an ambulance trip. It's the only way I can be confident he will actually get to the destination.

I wish him well and stress that medicine can get him back to reasonable health. I drive home later in silence. No NPR on the radio; I simply want quiet. I can't get the image of his face and all that death in the eighties out of my mind. So many young men lost. I wish we had done a better job for them.

I never see or hear from the couple again. I wish they could read my letter though, maybe send me an email with an update. I want to believe he found help and is living somewhere, happy and healthy.

PC

MY WIFE WON'T
GET OUT OF BED

Dear Jack,

I learn something new every single day in the ER. That is a big part of what has kept me fascinated with this practice over the years. Today, it was a reminder about the power of observation, about really looking at what is going on and trying to understand its relationship to the patient.

My patient was in room thirteen. Though I am not superstitious, I am reminded that many people are wary of this number. The chief complaint, written on the top of the chart, reveals little. It merely says my next patient won't get out of bed. I silently wonder what I will find.

As I enter the room, my patient, a seventy-five-year-old woman, is lying flat on her back, eyes open, and in no obvious distress. Her husband is sitting disinterestedly near the foot of the bed, reading a magazine. This strikes me as a bit odd, but perhaps he is just expecting a long wait and is getting comfortable.

I introduce myself and shake his hand, as is my practice, and turn to the patient. She looks like she is chronically ill, not emaciated, but rather thin. Her eyes are open, but she stares only at the ceiling and offers little response to my questions. This sort of presentation in the elderly is not uncommon. Some patients refuse to go the doctor until they are critical, while others come to the ER with a simple scratchy throat at 2 a.m. on a Saturday night. I wonder how long she has been like this and begin to question her husband, even before I have started my exam.

He says his wife has been ill for about a week. She has been refusing to get out of bed, even to eat. She has been taking fluids, however, so, he has made her chicken broth daily. The recalcitrance to call for a physician's help surprises me, but again, is sometimes common in the elderly. That's odd because they are precisely the group that should have a lower threshold for seeking health care. They're the ones at highest risk for real disease.

I learn my patient has had no fevers, chills, or falls. The rest of her medical history is really of little help. She is on the usual cocktail of medications, and right away I wonder if they are the cause. I have always been bothered by how often our medications contribute to problems instead of healing us. Before reaching for the prescription pad, we would do well to consider primum non nocere.

I start my exam and go from head to toe carefully. Her mental status is clearly abnormal. Her lips are cracked, and the back of her throat is dry, so, I naturally suspect she has some dehydration. There are no marks of prior trauma. Her breathing is a bit labored, and there are little crackles in her lungs that suggest maybe pneumonia. As I begin to examine her abdomen and pull down the bed sheet I find she has soiled herself with feces. I pull the sheet back up quickly and simply feel her abdomen. I find it soft and benign. Her extremities are all symmetrically weak. I am unsure of the cause at this time. The only other notable issue is her blood oxygen is a little low, showing ninety percent saturation on the monitor. I order a little nasal oxygen. I tell the husband I will be ordering lab and X-rays. He simply says, "Good."

As I walk back to the computer to enter orders, I call out to the nurse for a STAT blood sugar test. Blood glucose is one of the first things to treat if it is low and could be the cause of everything. I am also considering the differential diagnosis. This is what we call the list of possible problems that could explain this presentation. And in this case, it's long. I order routine labs, a sepsis screen, a catheterized urine sample, a CT scan of her brain and a portable chest X-ray. A few other tests as well. An infection or a stroke is high on my list right now. Both problems are all too common in this age group. I also ask the nurses to clean up the patient after giving them the bad news that she has soiled herself.

Her sugar level turns out to be a little low, fifty-eight instead of at least seventy. That's not enough to explain all of this, but I treat it anyway. She hasn't eaten solid food in a week, so I figure a little IV glucose won't hurt her. And then she is off to the radiology department.

An hour or so later, the studies I ordered return. A CT scan of the brain fails to show a stroke, hemorrhage, or fracture. I look it over myself. Once in a while, even the radiologist will miss something, and I have looked at thousands of scans. Similarly, I study the chest X-ray. There is no pneumonia. I am beginning to gravitate toward the possibility of a urinary tract infection as a cause. But the urinalysis returns pretty normal, except for high ketones from not having eaten for a week. Her other labs are pretty unremarkable, although they confirm dehydration. So, now it's a bona fide mystery. Why won't she get out of her bed? Why does she lie here now, semi-conscious, almost like she's sedated?

I speak further with the husband while the staff unceremoniously, though with dignity, remove all of her gowns and underwear to clean her. And there with the sheet off and her in her birthday suit I notice something I missed while she was gowned and under the sheet.

Her breathing pattern is highly abnormal. She is using abdominal and other accessory muscles to breathe. Now this is really odd. There are a number of causes for this, but with her presentation and with her weak extremities, I am suddenly concerned about a potential spinal cord problem. Has the blood supply to her spinal cord become impeded in some way? We place a cervical collar on her to help protect her neck from further injury. She is awake enough, responds to pain, and likely able to do this herself, but I put it on anyway. Even with no history of trauma, this protection is important. Maybe the paramedics who brought her or I should have done this at the start.

Spinal fractures can occur in this group with very little trauma. Bones in the spinal column that are riddled with osteoporosis simply collapse under the body's weight. Just how fragile the aged become scares me a bit.

I ask the husband again about falls. He says no, no falls. But she stumbled about ten days ago. She never hit the ground and didn't seem to hurt anything, he says. These collapses of weak vertebrae usually cause pain and disability but only rarely damage the spinal cord. It can happen, though. So I order a STAT portable cervical spine X-ray. Alarms are going off in my head as I put this all together. I have become convinced her problem is mainly neurological. The X-ray of her neck returns in just minutes and I can't believe what I see on the film.

My patients odontoid process, a piece of bone that sticks up from the second cervical vertebrae that both attaches our head to the neck and allows us to rotate are head, is broken clean off. Even worse, it is displaced, putting pressure on her spinal cord. And this explains everything. Everything except why the husband hasn't called for assistance much sooner. He insists his wife was fine a week ago, but surely, even the most recalcitrant among us would seek help if a fully normal spouse suddenly couldn't get out of bed.

I explain what I have seen to the husband, and he remains rather nonchalant, unsurprised, and rather disinterested. What the hell? Someone here has already called Adult Protective Services. Likely, one of the nurses. That call seems perfectly in order to me, and at this point, I would be making it myself. At any rate, protective services call, wanting to speak with me. Good. I tell them the story and they say they will come directly to the ER.

I order a CT scan of her neck. I really don't need it at this point, but I know the accepting neurosurgeon is going to want to see it. I also order blood gases. This test will tell me if she is acidotic or if carbon dioxide has accumulated in her blood. She is likely not breathing deeply enough to expel all of the carbon dioxide her body produces. When the level gets high enough, this can cause sedation. Jeez, this is becoming one bizarre ending to the complaint, "My wife won't get out of bed."

Her blood gas test returns, and I am embarrassed by the result. Her carbon dioxide is over ninety and should be around forty. I am shocked this wasn't more clinically apparent, as I had studied her respiratory pattern carefully. That is how I came to suspect a spinal cord problem. But there it is, right on the little piece of paper the respiratory tech brings to us each time we order a blood gas. Damn. I order a ventilator set up and ask the staff to prepare medications to put down a breathing tube. The ventilator will help her breathe better.

An intubation on a patient with an unstable neck fracture is a dangerous procedure. If not carefully done, you can displace the fracture further, causing even more damage. If you are especially unlucky, you can even sever the spinal cord. I love this job, but you can find yourself in the most precarious of positions. To help guard against making a bad situation worse, I will use a video-assisted scope to intubate. I will have other staff stabilize her head and neck while I do it and hope I can accomplish the task without moving her at all.

The intubation turned out to be a breeze. The breathing tube went right in. She didn't move at all. Within ten minutes of the intubation, the medication to paralyze her is wearing off. Now she is trying to pull out the breathing tube! We quickly restrain her arms to the bed and sedate her mildly. This is actually great news. Her spinal cord is working better than I thought, and most of her inability to move was sedation from that carbon dioxide build up.

The neurosurgeon accepts the transfer and we call the helicopter. In an hour or so she will be in the ICU. I am hopeful that her spine can be stabilized surgically and that she will return to her life. My part of her care is almost done.

A police detective appears to question me. He wants to know what I think about this. Did her husband break her neck? Or did he just neglect her in bed? Or was he just too unsophisticated to even realize there was such a major problem going on? I have no conclusions to offer. Any and all could have happened, I say, but I add that I do not think there is evidence he intentionally caused the injury.

As I hear the helicopter take off, I take a few minutes to again ponder how fate, or chance, plays such an unappreciated role in our lives. What if I hadn't noticed the strange way she was breathing? What if she had not soiled herself so I could even make the observation while the nurses cleaned her up? Without those two lining up just right under the stars, she likely would have been admitted to the floor for dehydration and maybe sepsis of an undetermined cause. What if? What if?

And that, Jack, is why I consider observation to be one of the most powerful tools in a doctor's bag. And sometimes I am both thankful and fearful of fate.

PC

THIS BABY IS CHOKING

Dear Jack,

It's a Sunday morning and still early and slow on my shift. Few will come to the ER early on Sundays, and here, not until after church is over. If there's an NFL game on, they'll try to squeeze that ER visit in between church letting out and the game. That's not always a great plan. Sometimes everyone else has the same idea, and they miss the entire game.

The EMS encoder tones out and I immediately hear the excited voice of a paramedic reporting a nine-month-old baby choking to death. The infant is gasping for air. The paramedic says he looked with a laryngoscope but couldn't see anything. The crew is using an Ambu bag, attempting to breathe for the baby. The bag is self-inflating, sort of like a collapsible ball with a hole in it, and attached to the hole is a facemask that fits over the nose and mouth of the patient. They will be here in minutes.

As we get the room ready and the staff assembled, I am thinking this may be an intimidating and difficult case. A pediatric airway obstruction can be tough and help from a colleague would be welcome. But it is Sunday, so it will be just me, most likely. I have a clerk call down to the OR to see if an anesthesiologist might be there but learn there is none. A doctor on-call today is at least half an hour away and will be of no help to me. It will all be over by then. Good or bad.

While we wait, I consider my role as an ER doctor and just how different it is from almost all other doctors. We work in uncontrolled circumstances. We are required by federal law to take all comers, from cradle to grave, no matter the problem. I am proud to be able to do this and be part of the emergency care system. It requires unique training and experience. You see, Jack, our expertise must be very broad, the polar opposite of specialists. They are very narrow in their capabilities, but their knowledge in their specific field is far deeper than ours. I see fewer doctors wanting to be in my position today. Even I am not too happy about being in the pit today to face the coming emergency.

The paramedics arrive, still using the Ambu bag and doing their best to hold down the struggling baby. I ask for a quick report and am told the mother thinks the baby swallowed a piece of plastic.

At times like this you have to struggle to keep your cool. I will show no outward signs of nervousness or a sense of panic to the staff. It's contagious. Everyone will do a better job the calmer I can keep my demeanor. I know this from experience.

I turn to my patient. We get him moved on to our gurney and the nurses go to work getting him on the monitor and an IV started. I find the baby to be wide-awake and ask the paramedic to stop bagging so I can check his respiratory efforts. He is breathing adequately. I hear the high-pitched, squeaky sound that comes with every breath, called stridor, but he is moving air. Good, I have a little time to think. I stop the bag ventilation and put the baby on humidified oxygen.

The stridor sound means there is some degree of upper airway obstruction. All parents who have had a small child with croup have heard this crowing sound. By its nature, it evokes fear and panic. A person struggling to breathe could be dying. It's not a comforting noise, but right now, I am glad to hear it. My patient and I are on thin ice, but it hasn't broken through yet. He is still breathing on his own.

The rest of my exam and the history obtained from Mom are unhelpful. As Mom did not actually see the baby swallow the plastic, I inquire about any upper respiratory symptoms the past twenty-four hours. This might just be a case of croup after all. But no, she says, no symptoms. No fever. Either way, I am not going to rush this. *Primum non nocere.* Rush things and I could accidentally force a foreign body deeper into the airway and then be unable to extract it. This would likely kill the baby. I also want to avoid moving too soon to paralyze the baby with drugs. I may not be able to ventilate the baby or get a breathing tube down successfully after he is paralyzed. That would be lethal. I order a breathing treatment with a medication that can reduce swelling in the airway. I also order IV steroids to help accomplish the same. I hope both will buy more time. A second IV as a backup would be good because of the chance of one coming out during a critical procedure. It can become difficult to start an IV in a baby as the situation worsens. No, I am going to measure every step and move slowly this time. It feels right.

The hospital head nurse has come down to help. As I leave the room briefly, she stops me and asks, "How can you be so calm with this going on?" I don't tell the truth, that I am not calm inside, at all. I answer, "Thirty-five years of taking care of babies. You learn thinking can be more important than acting." She nods.

We get some soft tissue neck X-rays to see if a foreign body shows up. Maybe there are telltale signs of croup. Either way, these images can be helpful.

The first nebulizer treatment helps somewhat. The baby is looking around the room, still stridorous but clearly in better shape. Good enough. I decide to let Mom hold the baby and calm him down. This isn't simply because I feel the baby should be comforted. I know the steady, easy breathing of a calm baby will help all of us. The infant airway is still very flexible, and when it's rapidly trying to breathe, this causes some negative pressure that can partially collapse the airway. I want everything I do to produce more room for air to move. I want this baby well oxygenated before taking any steps to paralyze him, remove the foreign object, and place a breathing tube. I order a second nebulizer treatment, just as I would for croup. I honestly am still not sure if I am dealing with an illness or a stuck object.

My X-ray returns and I do not see a foreign body. But plastic is notoriously hard to see on a plain X-ray. There are no clear signs of croup, either, and a baby in this much distress would most likely show some visible swelling on the X-ray film. I decide I will just have to take the next step and look down the throat with the laryngoscope. While the baby is still doing marginally Ok, and a little better, he won't be able to keep this work of breathing up for much longer. I'm just going to have to bite the bullet and proceed with getting this done.

The second neb has finished, and I now have the baby placed on the maximum amount of oxygen we can deliver. Blood has a very limited ability to store more oxygen than you use on a second to second basis, but the highest blood saturation I can get will buy me more time as try to remove the object and put the breathing tube down. I order medications for paralysis and sedation to be drawn up into a pair of syringes and get ready to administer them. I get a selection of airway tubes out, difficult airway aids, and Magill forceps. Magills are a special forcep that are angled, enabling them to reach down into the deeper throat and remove an object. They're also used to help guide a breathing tube between the vocal cords and into the trachea. All will be ready and at my grasp before I take the next step.

Taking away a patient's ability to breathe on his or her own is the most frightening thing I do medically. Once you stop a patient from breathing, it is all on you To place the tube or breathe for them with the Ambu bag. And we all deeply fear the circumstance of being unable to do either. It does happen. And the patient dies. Just like that. You have killed them with your attempt to help. You have violated *primum non nocere*.

As the staff finishes getting prepared I step out of the room for a minute to gather my courage, calm myself, and rethink the procedure. Am I doing the right thing? Have I thought of everything? Are the staff and I as ready as we can be?

Just moments before I am ready to head into the treatment room and start, literally, seconds before I am to give the orders to administer the drugs and roll the dice to save my patient, the baby has a significant coughing fit. I can hear it from outside the door. And then one of the nurses comes out of the room with his mouth agape and his eyes wide. In his hand, he is holding a present. A very welcome present.

He extends his hand to me and opens his palm. He is holding the piece of plastic. The baby has coughed the plastic up himself! A ragged chunk of blue plastic. The medications we gave likely reduced the swelling that can rapidly develop when an airway is traumatized. This made a little more breathing room and loosened the plastic that was wedged there. Hallelujah!

I offer Mom the plastic and leave to write in the chart. Always a chart to write. I simply will not be able to accurately reflect this morning's drama or describe my decision-making or how my experience guided me away from possibly creating an even more dangerous situation by acting too quickly. How being outwardly calm kept my team focused and prevented their panic. Maybe I'll just write, "Baby choked on plastic piece but then coughed it up." That will be easier.

As I am charting, the hospital charge nurse comes over. Her words are music to my ears. "I am glad it was you that was here today and being Mr. Cool, Calm, and Collected." And then goes back upstairs to assume her duties. She will never learn the real truth.

The rest of the day went by in a flash. You just can't spoil the mood I was in after this case. We saved a baby's life. We did it *a la primum non nocere*. There is nothing better, my friend.

PC

THE DREAM

Dear Jack,

Last night I had the dream again. I'm having it every three or four weeks for some reason. The same theme. We are back in college, studying for finals in the graduate school library. It's that large, stately room, with wood paneling on all the walls and ceiling. The room itself, with that scent of old wood, makes you believe it is an important place. Rows and rows of tables with an open isle down the center. All of those green legal style reading lamps sit on top of the tables, mostly off. It's very quiet here; the only sounds are pages turning, books closing, a muffled cough, or a chair being pushed one way or another. The library was the most serene place on campus. I loved studying there.

In the dream, we are in finals week. We get up for a study break to climb the hill to Latimer Hall and see how we did on the Chem 1 final. And then I shudder with terror. Suddenly I realize I have completely forgotten about an entire course I signed up for! What the hell have I been thinking? I don't even know what course it is. Was it another semester of rhetoric? An English lit class? The functional anatomy of frogs? I haven't a clue. I just know I was supposed to go to class, buy the books, and read them. But I have done nothing. Nada. And the final is Friday. I'm going to get an F.

I wonder if I drop everything else and simply focus on that one course for the next three days if I can pass it. I'll just go down to the bookstore and buy the class notes and the books, come back to the library and give it my undivided attention. I'm a good student and a quick learner. I tell myself it might be possible. It's too late to drop the course. That date had passed five weeks into the semester. But how can I prepare for a final when I can't even remember the name of the class? I'm just going to get that failing grade I fear so much. Somewhere on campus, posted on some unknown door this coming Monday, will be the computer printout we always look for, and it will say, "P. CROCKER – F".

This dream is different, though, and lacks the usual frustrating end. For some reason, I become lucid and think, "Why do I care about this course?" I've already graduated, completed my master's, and then went to medical school. This imagined failing grade from forty-five years ago simply doesn't matter anymore. I've even completed my full thirty-seven-year clinical career and am retired. It's time to let my fear of this failure go. Its opportunity has come and gone. This forgotten course I dream of, this imagined failure, is completely irrelevant. Just an illusion.

I know this is a common anxiety dream that people have about being unprepared for something. But I wonder if its meaning changes throughout one's life. I also wonder if my version of this dream is actually about something else. Once upon a time, it really was about that college course I forgot to attend. Now, perhaps, it's about realizing what time it is in my life. It's not the sunset, at least I hope not, but it is late afternoon. And I fear it's later than it seems.

As long as you have your health, time marches silently on, unnoticed. Even your face in the mirror as you brush your teeth doesn't seem to change that much. Until you see an old picture. And then it strikes you. Is that what I looked like? I looked like a kid. I had hair. My beard was jet black and now almost white. Where did all of that time go?

I never thought I would save the world, but maybe there was something I was supposed to have accomplished that I haven't yet, something important left for me to do. Perhaps the dream is now a reminder that there are still things to do. I have no rigid schedules, no structured classes to worry me. But something inside me says I need to get busy while there is still time. I simply don't know what is. And I fear not figuring it out, getting that failing grade.

PC

P.S. The song Time by the Chamber's Brothers has been stuck in my head since the dream. You remember that song that speaks of choosing your own path while young, not caring what others say, finding YOUR path. And then coming to a new understanding of time has been revealed to you and that it is that time that has come. It completely captures my mood.

Do you remember the first word of that song? Listen to it carefully. That IS life.

EPILOGUE

Dear Reader,

I hope you enjoyed these snapshots of notable cases that occurred during the course of my career. It seems impossible to reduce a practice that encompassed approximately 150,000 patients and thirty-seven years into just 40 clinical vignettes, but I did my best. As you can imagine there were many other equally fascinating encounters. Encounters that kept my career mesmerizing.

I have been asked about the structure of the book as a series of apparently disconnected patient encounters without an apparent overlying theme. An emergency physicians career is experienced in just this fashion, a seemingly endless progression of vignette encounters with patients. No follow up, never knowing how their story ends. No continuity of care. And for those cases involving critical illness or injury we never even get to finish the case and often do not learn the outcome. In a sense it is a career without an overarching theme. The first few hours of critical care is our province and then the patient is gone from our lives. This is perhaps the greatest weakness of the specialty. The vignette experience of your work life is a perspective that can bleed into your personal affairs and can create a sense of disassociation in how you experience other life events. Family life after all is a continuous enduring progression not experienced in disconnected bits and pieces.

Chapter 3, **The Pecking Order**, is one that also garnered a number of comments from test readers. Some felt it was too long and no longer represents the training experience in medicine, while others felt it offered a real inside look at resident life. Regardless, it is the milieu I was trained in and also one of the original letters that was recoverable. While I did edit it down I felt it was important to include it in as close to the original text as reasonable. To be fair, the environment of today's trainees is quite different. Training hours and work demands have been limited to help provide for safer patient care, eliminate most sleep deprivation, and generally improve what remains a grueling experience. The relationships between trainees and mentors is much more collegial today. And there are fewer sharks in the water these days, but they do remain, at least in the waters of Emergency Medicine. And they do need to be dealt with.

To survive in the emergency environment you must learn some unique skills. Skills that do not come naturally, the basics of which are not taught in books or medical school. Skills only learned on the front line, when a patient outcome depends upon you. Times when you must depend on yourself and your decisions as much as the patient depends upon you. The most unnatural of these is making decisions with limited information. And making quick decisions that do or don't save lives. You also learn you must have faith in the path you chose; there is little room for self-doubt during a major emergency. Woulda, shoulda, coulda, will get you nowhere. Live with the reality of what is, not what might have been. Then deal with the situation to the best of your ability. You become used to the revelation that for you there is never time for certainty. And always the need for multitasking, never able to focus on just one thing without interruption as ten things are going on at once all around you all of the time. The constant interruptions, influx of information, and requests become an unwelcome but unavoidable blare in your brain.

As I walked out the door and away from my last shift I felt good. I had a great career but it was time for something new, different. A new chapter as a rancher. Though I loved the practice of medicine immensely there were no regrets or thoughts of taking part-time work to keep my hand in. Simply a clean break and a new page. There was however a certain sense of ennui. Perhaps because I now realized at this point in life time itself might be my most precious commodity. Only so many sunrises remain. Also a sense that something unknown has been left undone, similar to *The Dream* chapter in the book. Something important. Maybe it was writing this book and sharing my experiences. A catharsis of sorts. And this added fuel to ruminations and commitment to write this book.

In retrospect was it the correct career choice?

For me the answer is an unequivocal yes. I loved the excitement, the intermittent chaos, and the camaraderie that comes with being part of a team that works side-by-side to save lives. Nothing could have been better than helping patients by solving their medical puzzles and getting them back to good health when it was possible. But did I give up too much? Did I ask my family to give up too much?

For those imagining that practice in the emergency room might be an exciting lifestyle the answer may be surprising. The life of the emergency physician only vaguely resembles TV portrayals. Being part of a team that staffs a 24/7/365 emergency department can be grueling. The work schedule itself a challenge that defies your natural circadian rhythms and can make an absolute mess of trying to lead a normal family life. Half or more of your work shifts will be evening shifts during normal family time, or all-nighters while your family sleeps comfortably at home. And the next day you must sleep and miss more of your family's life. Eight continuous hours of sleep daily is a rarity. Half of all your holidays will be spent in the ER working. For many this disrupted life style, along with dealing daily with severe illness, trauma, grief, and the deaths we witness, can take its toll. Your family will sacrifice for your career.

It can be a career choice that leads to early professional burn out and leads some on a search for solace through drugs and alcohol. A series of broken relationships and disconnection from family and friends are not uncommon. If you cannot find that balance between providing comfort and care to the ill and injured while at the same time maintaining some emotional distance it can destroy you. Deaths occurring right before you, sometimes with contributions of your own hand through a clinical misstep or a care plan for a patient that doesn't work out as expected. These can consume you.

Not unique to EM are the medical failures. Or what feel like failures. Patients that didn't respond to the care you thought was best. There are always a number of paths to take. Although all may be medically acceptable sometimes you discover one doesn't work out as expected. Your patient fails to respond, worsens, may even die. There are always deaths. But also saves. Always complications. But also great successes. It all balances out somehow, though you are left with the constant feeling that maybe you could have done more. Performed better. Outcomes are not in your hands though it feels like they are. This unavoidably leads to a sense of responsibility for every outcome and every patient that you care for. This weighs upon you constantly.

And of course there is always the BIG QUESTION looming over your shoulder. You must accept complications will occur, mistakes will be made, and despite all of your efforts toward primum non nocere patients will suffer and some will die. You will at times cause harm. And you will feel as though you have fallen hard, failed your patient, and failed yourself.

So, can you get up and carry on afterwards? That is the BIG QUESTION. Not just finish a bad shift but continue to face this reality throughout a lengthy career. That is the question and the challenge of emergency medicine. After you fall can you get up? It's not for everyone.

PC

P.S. If you don't know the song listen to ***These Days***, by Jackson Browne. A beautiful melancholy lament about later in life realizing all the things you forgot to do and all the times you had the chance to do them. It's time to do them now.

To know my heart today, listen to the song.

ACKNOWLEDGEMENTS

I am forever grateful to my wife Marcia and daughter Alison. They made my career possible, and hence, this book, through their unfailing support of everything I wanted to pursue in medicine. My many absences from home and important events in their lives required sacrifices on their part and a generosity of spirit that awed me. Although many years have passed, I cannot adequately thank Jack Coakley, my good friend who encouraged me throughout college and inspired this book. My brother Tim Crocker also has been my sounding board and a great listener. He can now read some of the stories I never told and understand what I did with my life. I am also grateful for my high school teacher Scott Graff. He taught me basic chemistry and physics. More importantly, he taught me how to teach myself. I was lucky to have been his student.

Special thanks to TJ Milling, M.D., Don Connell, M.D., JoAnn Dawson (author), and Will Clementson, D.O., who went above and beyond offering their time, expertise, and invaluable comments. And to all of my test readers: John McManus, M.D., Tory Meyer, M.D., Heather Moeser, Rene Teeler, Tim Crocker, Travis and Cindy Pipkin, Kenneth Shine, M.D., Sharon Long, M.D., Bob Schlechter,.M.D., Joy Selak (author), Stephen Harrigan (author), Jalaane Levi-Garza and Dan Garza, Ben Brieger, M.D., Bill Fowler, Art Zeitz, and Jon Aultschuld. Mike Levy (Founder of **Texas Monthly**) for expert advice on publishing. Thanks as well to Marc Swender for the cover photo.

Finally I want to thank my editor, Mary Ann Roser (roser@roserprose. com). Although she never got to complete the editing to her satisfaction her encouragement, kind words and thoughtful editing made this a better book. The errors in print that remain are my own.

PC

I SINCERELY HOPE YOU ENJOYED THIS BOOK. THE BOOK HAS BEEN INDEPENDENTLY PUBLISHED SO THERE ARE NO MAJOR PUBLISHERS INVOLVED, AND NO FORMAL PROMOTION OR MARKETING. I AM DEPENDING ON THOSE READERS WHO LIKE THE BOOK TO SEND A RECOMMENDATION TO FIVE OF THEIR FRIENDS. IT IS THROUGH YOUR CONNECTIONS ON SOCIAL MEDIA THAT YOU CAN HELP GET THESE STORIES TO INTERESTED READERS.

LET YOUR FRIENDS KNOW THE PREFERRED BOOKSELLER IS THE BOOKBABY ON LINE STORE [bookbaby.com]. IT IS ALSO AVAILABLE ON 50 OTHER INTERNET SELLERS.

THANK YOU.

P.C.